Wipε Out
a true story of winning

Mary

Love JN 3:16

Follow 1 Corinth 11:1

Trust Prov 3:5

"Our Town" ... may the

God who cares so much

about us richly bless

you, your husband and

kids &

At last! This was a story waiting to be written. The tragic events described in this book actually happened. But injustice didn't make Dave Walden bitter—it made him better. God used life circumstances to get a playboy's attention and change him into an outstanding, honest, and humble servant among those whom God loves the most. This story will change the lives of those who read it.

Brian Winslade, Senior Pastor
Windsor Park Baptist Church
Auckland, New Zealand

The tears in my eyes make it difficult to read the words in his memoir. It may be due to a friendship beginning in the late 1970s that felt more like a "brotherhood," or it may be the stark and poignant reality that this story of life, love, and redemption is true. I choose to say that it is all of this and then some. If you want to read a story that is about personal discovery and love, then this is the book for you. David Walden's path led him on a journey that most of us can only imagine, but *Wipe Out* is not just a story for those who have experienced challenges. Take the time to read one man's account of his odyssey as he travels from success and abundance into the darkness—and then re-emerges into the light.

Stephen L. Bruce, President
Seal Beach Financial Center

Wipe Out is a compelling narrative told with complete honesty which holds the reader's interest from the first to the last page! My husband and I each read it in one sitting.

We couldn't put it down once we started. We know David personally through our association with him as hospital chaplains, but we had never before heard his personal testimony in such detail. His is a true story of a life transformed by the power, love, and mercy of God! May his story influence many lives.

Sharon Sotelo, Assistant Chaplain
Pomerado Hospital and Villa Pomerado

Wipe Out is the story of a Jonah who emerged from the giant fish and headed for Nineveh with new resolve. It is also the story of God's triumph in and through the unending adventure that is Dave's life and ministry. Dave has all the joyous, hopeful, and redemptive qualities of a man who is prepared to pour out his life for so many others. His readers will no longer be on the verge of a "wipe out," but on their way to a "lift-off"!

Dr. Don Buteyn
Honorable Retired, Senior Pastor,
Missions Director of the Presbyterian Church,
Former Dean, San Francisco Theological Seminary

Wipe Out is the story of a God who pursues us despite our brokenness—a God who is ever so willing to redeem the pieces of our lives and put us back together again. David reminds us that it is our natural tendency to build upon the sand: a foundation that crumbles under pressure. In contrast to the pursuit of *self*, David directs his reader to the transcendent significance and joy that comes through focusing on *others—*

especially on the disenfranchised and powerless in our midst. It is a pleasure to recommend this inspiring book that I found hard to put down. I trust that those who don't know David will have the same experience. I'm purchasing copies for each of my three sons.

Kent A. Eaton, PhD
Associate Dean and Professor of Pastoral Ministry
Bethel Seminary San Diego

Chappy Dave is one of the most dedicated Christians I know of. This book provides a historical vantage point for seeing his progress and accomplishments. Not only does it point out low and high points of his journey, but it can also provide great inspiration to all of us in our day-to-day struggles.

Bill Eisenecher
Entrepreneur, Retired CEO

Dave Walden's moving story is a truly welcome reminder of what the Lord can do in the life of anyone willing to deny self, take up the cross, and follow him wherever he leads.

Dr. Ronald Youngblood
Emeritus Professor of Old Testament
Bethel Seminary San Diego

DEDICATION

To John "Mac" Carroll McColister (1917-1999), a mentor in work ethics, for being down-to-earth where the salt, dirt, and sweat come together. Mac made the most of his time as a productive, prosperous family man who fished with zeal and loved his adopted children. Even without a formal education, Mac went the extra mile to care for widows, working hard at four jobs to make it happen, without boasting. Mac taught me to multitask, something intellectuals call "being an entrepreneur." By his example, Mac taught this 21-year old son-in-law the value of integrity. He showed me and everyone who knew him the meaning of "Man of God." Mac was my mentor, my hero, my friend.

CONTENTS

PART TWO
Chappy

FOREWORD
BY MOTHER ANTONIA

Dear Reader,

Pastor David has given me a great honor and also a difficult task: to write an introduction to the story of his life. I dedicated a day to spending time alone in a monastery where I reflected on Pastor David and his story. I hope in some way to give him the honor he deserves, and I'm going to write from my heart so I don't diminish the value of our own wonderful, Christ-like friendship that we have had for 12 years since 1994.

It is my decision to not be affected or swayed with accolades or criticisms surrounding the life of a man I have come to know and trust as a missionary co-worker in the vineyard of Our Lord where God is disguised as a prisoner. I appreciate and love the heart and spirit of Pastor David, and because one letter cannot relate so many years of experiences, I will tell you just a little bit of the reason why.

I am a Catholic Sister, who for 30 years has also been blessed to know and love the rejected Christ among those who have been wounded and have wounded others. Most prisoners around the world are *not* there for heinous crimes, although no criminal act is a good thing. You would find that the common denominator is poverty and ignorance. And sadly, there are those people who are innocent and have no way of proving it.

Please try to place yourself in a prison, not in one made of fear, ambition or unforgiveness, but in a prison made of cells and bars, a place of justice in the eyes of many, and injustice in the hearts of others. Here is where I first encountered this Shepherd of the Lord.

He is not just a shepherd, he is a "Good Shepherd" who loves the "sheep" God has sent him, men and women who are eventually transformed by the overpowering Holy Spirit-filled Pastor who brings the great kindness of the Lord to everyone he meets.

Even when he could not enter La Mesa Penitentiary because he was not on the master list, he brought many carloads of clothes, Bibles, and food to Casa Campos de San Miguel (a Catholic home for women which is close to the prison) so that I could bring them to anyone in need. It was not important to Pastor David if the women thought the supplies were from a Catholic Sister. It was important to him to keep giving, and for the needy to receive.

And again before he was allowed to come into prison, he would drive down to Tijuana and walk around the prison—praying—just like Joshua had walked around the walls of Jericho before capturing that city. The prison walls surely came down for Pastor David, too. And he is still with us on the inside. Praise God!

We both respect the Christian faith and so we want our behavior to be pleasing to God. When I know that a prisoner in search of spiritual peace is not a Catholic, I happily send him to Pastor in good faith. Very often we worked on cases together to help pay the bail, or to contact the news or a prisoner's family.

It seems to me that it would be better for one of the hundreds of prisoners Pastor David helped to be writing this. Someone such as Enrique, who is stricken with AIDS. His eyes sparkle when he tells me of his encounters with Christ through Pastor Dave: "I feel the profound forgiveness of the mercy of Christ in Pastor Dave." This is because of his Bible teaching, or even more, because of his biblical living.

Margaret was a victim of heroin and prostitution but is now living a free and a good life thanks to Pastor Dave, who still keeps in touch with Maggie to keep her on the road to Him who is the Way.

In Pastor David I have encountered the essential qualities of a true minister of Christ: Pastor David is the one who serves the others by spiritually washing their feet. And all that he does is with joy. I have never seen him angry or hostile. Never have I heard Pastor David speak ill of anyone, nor have I ever heard anyone speak ill of him.

So you see, my judgment is neither prejudiced nor my strictly own personal opinion. It is the collective opinion about a beloved man and servant of God!

Pastor David is always radiant with the light of the world that is so absolute and indentured in him by God's grace. May he light up your lives with the story of his life. May it encourage, inspire, and bless you.

Pastor David, may you remain always the meek and humble of heart man of God that you are. This old lady has been on the run, and I know that your prayers and your love and your guidance have helped to sustain me. Thank you for being my friend. God Bless You.

"By this sign all men will know you: you will love one another as I have loved you."

With gratitude and prayers.
Peace, Love, Mercy,
Mother Antonia Brenner
May 1, 2006

Read more about this saint in her biography,
Prison Angel: Mother Antonia's Journey from Beverly Hills
to a Life of Service in a Mexican Jail *(Penguin, 2005)*
by Mary Jordan and Kevin Sullivan

PROLOGUE:
THANK YOU, FATHER
BY DAVID WALDEN

How many multimillionaires end up bankrupt…only to find true fulfillment as a servant?

How many men come out of the prison system labeled a "felon" with no money, no friends, no connections…and succeed in rebuilding a life?

How many people try to kill themselves…and live?

I know rebirth, and I'm living it now.

People have listened to my story, and I think most of them have believed me. Even those who didn't wanted to hear more. And over the years, people told me to write my story. A friend even started to write it down years ago—and that was before things really exploded.

But I thought, "Everyone has a story, and mine is just another one." It finally dawned on me that not everyone has been a Hollywood mogul, a chauffer-driven CEO in a limousine, the president of a successful TV and film production company, an executive producer, a world-class racing promoter, and a professional race car driver at the same time—especially not someone who in the midst of it all held a gun to his head wanting to leave this planet.

And it would be highly unlikely for that same person to dedicate the rest of his life to serving poor and broken people in prisons, hospitals, orphanages, and the inner city.

Writing *Wipe Out* has given me an opportunity to reflect on and summarize over 7,000 pages of court transcripts from my trial—'cause who the heck wants to read court transcripts?! I was born, equipped, trained, and tested by fire to plant my feet at this spot on earth: here and now. That's my life in a nutshell.

And I feel younger, more alive, and ready to ride the next wave every morning when I wake up and say, "Oh boy, oh boy, what's next, God? What's going to happen today? I can hardly wait to find out whom I will help, even if it only means offering a word of encouragement. Help me make this world better. Surprise me, God."

Hey, I'm no St. Paul, but I can relate to what happened 2,000 years ago on the road to Damascus in Syria. He heard an audible voice from heaven that said, "Why are you persecuting Me?" These words transformed a religious fundamentalist who was bent on arresting and even killing people of "The Way" into a regenerated man with a new purpose: serving the One he had been persecuting. God tapped me on the shoulder, too, and said, "You have heard me, now love others!"

So get ready. In the pages ahead, you're in for an entrepreneurial adventure that is relevant, transcending, and best of all...true. I did it, and I am doing it. *Whew.*

If only for one person, I'll tell my story, and if it can lift someone out of the hole and teach a practical lesson from real life as it's lived in the dirt, that would be cool. Oh, it's a fast read, too, with short chapters.

I'll admit...I made a lot of money. I was a successful financial planner, a visionary of future investment trends. I've thought about my entrepreneurial side in relation to this book. Am I out for personal gain? If that's the case, I pray that my motives will be straightened out, but I think I'm being honest with myself when I say that I am no longer comfortable being in the spotlight for my own glory.

My story is not a commercial enterprise. I want to thank

the loving Creator who saved my life. Chalk it up as one of the paradoxes from someplace lofty and divine: I can write a book about myself, that isn't really about me. It's about a new life that was handed to me when I wanted to die. It's about turning the focus away from me and onto the source of what the world calls the "Higher Power."

It's hard for you to know the heart of a character in a book, and my hope is that you remember my brokenness more than my success. God made my personality and I'm a frontliner, a leader on the edge, where a certain amount of independence is needed. If I wait until I'm perfected, I would never tell my story, so forgive me if I come across as puffed up—you're right, it's there. The pride is still being chipped away, and it will be a life-long process. I've been broken and I know what brokenness is. But I'm a sinner saved by grace.

Every life is unique and irreplaceable. I hope that by reading this book, others will hear the voice of love in their own lives and be transformed. I'll consider this book a worthy project only if it shows that the power of love is real. It actually wipes out failure, depression, rejection, loneliness, incarceration, death, you name it...and lets you rise on a new wave and drop in for the good fight.

I hope you'll feel the experience of riding a perfect, shoulder-high wave at La Jolla Shores as the sun rises over the glassy sea. You won't wipe out, you won't even get wet. As I would tell a surfer buddy heading out for a set, "I hope you get locked in and have a great session with each chapter!" Whether you're a longboarder who has lived for decades and has endured many joys and sorrows, or a shortboarder, still in your youth and living in the fast lane, you're literally in for the ride of a lifetime.

ACKNOWLEDGMENTS

I am blessed with the many great teachers who graced and enriched the classroom of this "created-in-the-image" human life. They taught me what they could within the time they were given.

There is first and foremost my wife, Sandee "da Boop," from whom I've learned the invaluable lesson of how to be a best friend: it's not how much you say it or know it—it's how much you show it. She would say to me, "Love is active in caring for others above yourself," and for that gift, I am richly rewarded. I am blessed to have her as my life partner in family and personal matters, in addition to being my trusted spiritual prayer leader in all matters of living and serving God.

To my children, Vincent Michael (along with Kelli and the kids, Parker and Connor) and Jessica Anna (and Peter), I offer you this, "You're in my heart…in my soul.…You'll be my friend 'til I grow old." My father, Don, who challenged me to further my education and his father, George "Pop" Walden, who launched me into the entrepreneurial world at age 14. Pop was my business mentor who introduced me to the importance of praying with my wife every day. Mom, Helen, whose love of life, kids, God, and me is immeasurable.

Then there is Dr. Pam Fox Kuhlken who is my colleague in communicating the truth of God's amazing grace and redemptive plan. I could not do what I do without her doing what she does so very well. I am overwhelmed by the grateful acknowledgments I receive from readers of *Wipe Out*. I usually smile and say, "I know." Pam is a world-class person like the world-class champions I sponsored and wrote about in the book.

My academic colleagues at Bethel University and Seminary, San Diego and St. Paul, Minnesota, teach and mentor me in the lesson of focused living. They continuously encourage me to reach out, look in, and press on—enhancing the journey of life God has provided me. I am thankful for their guidance and patience with me as one who is leading on the edge and outside-the-box of tradition. Professor Tom Correll, anthropologist and ethnographer, is a giant in the missiological field of "not-making-Roundsville-square." Author and professor, Dr. Ronald Youngblood, taught me humility, laughter, and appreciation for antiquity. Dr. Kent Eaton listened and offered sage advice. Professor Mark Strauss, author and scholar, taught me the mission of the church and the science of interpreting the Bible, and gave me a clearer understanding of "complementarianism," women as church leaders.

Dr. Don Buteyn, professor emeritus, taught me to go into "Our Town" and care for the least of these because that was doing it unto the One who gave the greatest of all gifts. Don, you and your wife, Marion, poured yourselves out to disciple thousands like me to become like Jesus. I am blessed to be counted with so many to have been mentored by you.

My undergraduate Bible and spiritual leader, Pastor Chuck Smith, demonstrated to me what faith looked like, vacuuming the conference hall at 6:00 a.m. before his students would arrive. My beloved friend and mentor, Pastor Jeff Jackson, thank you! Jeff, you believed in me and you kept me focused on moving "upward, inward, outward."

My attorney through the trial of the 1980's, Todd Landgren, gave himself and all his resources to represent me and my family. Todd, I never did give you all that you were due. You are a very special friend, and I will never be able to repay you. Your professional skills as a securities and trial lawyer are world-class. Your integrity and thoroughness did not go unnoticed. Thank you.

To my friends, Stephen Bruce and Richard Mills, whom I love closer than brothers, your visits to me in prison exemplified the true love of the One who calls us "friends." Stephen, my Jewish brother in the Lord, you are my best male friend. Thank you for always being there for me. Richard, your spirit departed this earth way too early, but your zeal for the love of *sophia* (wisdom) inspired me to seek and learn from her.

Sharon "Spurgeon" Sotelo, you are a marvelous woman of God. Thank you, Ralph Sotelo, her husband for nearly 50 years, for permitting me the time to learn to pray from your precious "strawberry blond" Sharon.

My MOTE advisory board reminded me to look out the window more. Ken Gerard, my friend and wise legal counselor, holds me accountable every week and is always there to offer me "Phila-delphia." And thanks to my sister in the faith, Lori Burnell, RN, MRSN, who believed in me and helped me get started in establishing faith-based missions within secular institutions.

My co-laborer at La Mesa Prison, Mother Antonia, taught me how to persevere in love and kindness in all circumstances. Mother, you are my role model in meekness. I call it the "power of God under control." Thank you for accepting me as a fellow servant of Christ. You taught me the value of commitment. Like you, I serve in an unorthodox way. Your calling came directly from God as you donned a nun's habit you sewed yourself to become "Mother Antonia." I, too, put on my clergy shirt, donned the collar, and entered into La Mesa as "Pastor David." Mother, Calvary Chapel rolled its eyes when they saw me wearing my collar. Thank God we are outside the box because that is where Jesus went!

I am blessed with the employees and partners with whom I have worked and currently work today. In the formative years of the business empire, I learned from so many contributors of talent and time. My executive assistant, Ladora Buck, taught me time management and how to stay connected to co-workers as though they were family. James Cavanaugh introduced me to competitive racing and fun. Mr. B taught me a most difficult lesson that led me to real life here and now and forever. Roger Riddell gave me hope in the middle of crisis.

Bruce Brown shared his talent with me by allowing me to participate with him in the simple pleasure of seeing life through the motion picture lens, watching friends and family laughing, engaged in surfing or motorcycles in our film, *On Any Sunday II.*

The teams of volunteers from the San Diego area as well as the collaborative friends of MOTE have helped all of this come together. Tom Miller is a creative genius. His giftedness with computer creativity put the mission of MOTE on the map and he did it out of love and gratitude. Marilyn Machen, administrative assistant and grandmother of 11, cannot be appreciated enough. Kathy Johnson, entrepreneur extraordinaire, and her recently departed and precious husband, Dick, taught me devotion and love for the homeless.

In Carol Fore, my gifted friend, I see the hand of God through gentleness. Thank you, Carol, for all you did in assembling and editing my doctoral dissertation.

God sent me Coni McCall just at the right time. Thank you for giving yourself to the ministry with your editing and executive administrative support.

A mentor once spoke these words to me: "The value of one's life can only be measured by what it has meant to others." Without all of you, this "new creation" made in the image of the living God would never exist.

Thanks to each and every one of you for giving me so much. Going from *wipe out* to *winning* is like being in the barrel of the wave: "Catch a wave and you're sitting on top of the world." When I focus on that which is eternal and not temporal, my life throttle is in sixth gear and I am not looking back, but pressing on to win.

PART
ONE

MIKEY

Scene One
Looking Back

{2006 ... 1984}

I
HUMILIATION IS...

Flies swarm around seven prisoners linked by chains around their wrists and ankles. They exit a bus at Chino State Prison and find themselves surrounded by cow pastures. The sheriffs unshackle and strip the prisoners naked so they can be hosed down. Getting within one inch of the prisoners' faces, the sheriffs scream for three hours at the top of their lungs, "You dirt bags have no rights! You're the property of the State of California, so screw you! You blink wrong and you'll be nailed!"

At that moment...I understood humiliation.

I was taken from the Emergency Room of Hoag Hospital in Orange County to a new destiny: Chino State Prison, known for its brutality, where Mexicans and blacks— members of such infamous gangs as the "Bloods" and "Crips"—exchanged frequent knifings using sharpened broomsticks. White guys kept a low profile, if you know what I mean, and the guards had to be hard, so they were in your face.

The prisoners would serve out their sentences and sell their souls to the state—only to be released and then hunted and branded on account of the very crimes they were expiated from. Forgiveness doesn't happen in a bureaucracy. Papers aren't shredded and accusations aren't erased, at least not by the winners holding the gavels and signing state budgets and keeping their jobs as public servants.

Picture this: a loading dock with a row of naked, big, bad-looking men, a few are black, a few are brown, all of them are covered in tattoos up and down every body part. In their midst is the hide of a clean-cut white dude who was CEO of one of the largest tax and financial planning businesses in Orange County. All of them are equally stripped, hosed down, and mentally screwed.

This couldn't be happening to me. How on earth did I get here? I was on that bus and now I'm standing naked on this dock dripping wet and verbally trashed. But this isn't really happening to me...or is it? Are the guards right? Is my business suit, my Rolex, and my life...now theirs?

Over 20 years later, that Caucasian man who is still me is standing on a table for visibility facing a similar group of prisoners in a Mexican penitentiary—some are American, but most are Mexican. I'm standing beside my interpreter shouting before a large crowd of 1,500 men and women:

You know what, guys? Been there, done that. I'm a C-number from Chino State Prison: C-194. I understand what you are talking about, buddy. Not fun.

¿Saben qué muchachos? Yo he estado en la misma situación. Yo soy parte de la numeración C de la prisión de Chino, C-194. Yo entiendo muy bien de lo que hablan y no es nada divertido.

"But gee," you say, "this is Mexico, an even tougher place than Chino," right? Listen, I understand that human beings do not do well being locked up: watching visitors leave, hearing the freeway outside their cell.

Ustedes se preguntarán "Pero aquí estamos en México un lugar mucho más difícil que en Estados Unidos que no?" Escuchen, entiendo que ningún ser humano se siente bien tras las rejas mientras miren que visitantes llegan y luego se van a sus casas o al oír desde su celda el sonido de carros en la vía rápida.

I recognize how difficult it is for you, but prison is prison. I was on the inside looking out, too.

Yo reconozco lo difícil que ha de ser, pero la prisión es lo que es, una prisión. Yo también estuve en tu lugar, mirando hacia afuera.

2
ACTION!

Having been a movie producer, it's ironic that I see my life as a screenplay. Mastershot: Chino. Zoom in: Loading dock. Stripped. Trashed. Humiliated. Fade out. Mastershot: La Mesa State Penitentiary in Mexico. A bankrupt multimillionaire brings food and clothes to men, women, and children abandoned in hell. Meeting needs. A light shining in the darkness. A refuge. Fade out.

But fading to visual darkness doesn't address the complexities of that transition. You're left wondering, *How in the world did a guy like that survive in Chino? Why has he returned to a new kind of service in a Mexican prison?*

As I write today, it's October 12, 2005, the 21st anniversary of my trial. When I stopped playing the role of "CEO-who-didn't-make-a-move-without-his-attorneys," suddenly, my life script made sense, but I can only see that in retrospect. Sure, there was the courtroom drama, but most of the action happened on the inside, on the edge of every known comfort zone. It was the edge of risk-taking that makes a surf dog like me say "Cowabunga"— even though it's become a cliché used only by poseurs and Hollywood, or rather, Hollyweird.

All I can do is reproduce the screenplay as I was called to live it: the wild ride that led to a "wipe out" in the best and worst sense of the word. I lost everything, then everything was erased and I surfaced from the deep. I got a second chance.

Do you ever feel like you're coasting, driving with your foot lightly on the gas, just cruising, never even hitting a red light or pothole? Or hang-gliding on a breezy afternoon, soaring like a seagull without an obstacle in the world? That's what riding a wave is like.

And if my life was a wave, I wiped out big time. My life was stained red from so many accusations and wounds, it blazed like the most intense crimson sunset, and then suddenly, it was a glassed-out crystal sea that would lull a baby to sleep. The wipe out was wiped out by love. Now every wave takes me to the next peak, and I'm still riding the set of a lifetime. I just haven't hit shore yet.

I'm getting ahead of myself.

SCENE TWO
HAPPY DAYS

{The 1950s}

3
SECOND PLACE
IS FOR LOSERS

I was born with a surfboard on my back (at least that's how I remember it) in San Diego's Mercy Hospital, 1949.

At eight years old in Hermosa Beach by the old pier, I climbed onto a surfboard and met up with all the surf doggies of the time. There were only a few. There were no crowds in 1959.

We lived the reality of the TV sitcom *Happy Days* (1974-84) and heard the Beach Boys play live at parties. "Catch a wave and you're sitting on top of the world, ooh wah, ooh wah...." Life felt like one giant peak.

I was a good surfer and president of the Bay City Surf Club for three years. I was an athlete who didn't like second place so I tried to be the best by doing extra push-ups, running extra laps—whatever it took to win.

And I did win. We won CIF in football. I was the fastest runner in school, and the CIF champion who set the junior varsity record for shot put my freshman year. I still pack the form, the style, the explosion!

In my senior year of high school, I recall a varsity game against Westminster High, which was a bigger school with monster-sized tackles who were 230 pounds. I weighed 165, but I was fast and liked to hit. The opposing giants were defending the goal lines, and I got the ball and went right through the center, diving underneath a sea of bodies all piled up in the end zone.

I was quick and small enough to fit underneath this dome of 20 guys who weren't even touching me. Then I crawled out through the gap and looked back at them, "Touchdown!" This happened because my attitude was "just give me the ball, coach."

I would plead with the coach, "Just give me the ball, give me the ball, give me the ball, coach! I'll run and score the touchdown, just give me the ball, coach, I'll run right through them. People get hit, no problem—just give me the ball, coach!"

Talk about leadership—this began my journey. I was being molded to achieve by excellent mentors: first by my coaches and then by my grandfather. It's easy to throw in the towel, but to be first string, you have to run extra bleachers and earn your place. I wouldn't give up. I started the race to win and finished the race believing I won even if I placed second. I won in my mind and my heart. That was me.

4
UNHAPPY DAYS
{DOREEN}

My two brothers and I adored our little sister, Doreen, who was the treasure of the house. When I was nine, she was just two. She loved to dance and sing in front of the TV looking just like Shirley Temple with her blond curls. (In 1957, TVs were large boxes with very few programs to watch, and what was available was perfectly suitable for children.)

Doreen was always smiling. Her spirit was so electric and inspiring that it moved our young hearts just like the children from Sunday School lessons who jumped onto the lap of Jesus when he said, "Let them come!" We loved being near Doreen.

The next thing I remember about Doreen was that when she was 2 ½ years old, she snuck out of the house alone, ran into the street, and was hit by a car. I think the most devastating part was that mom and dad were in the ambulance carrying little Doreen when she died...right in their arms. I realized even then how it impacted them beyond understanding.

My mother had a nervous breakdown and my father turned within. He must have been angry at God, and at just about everybody. He closed up and became cynical. He didn't drink or use drugs, he was just bitter. I was the middle of three sons, but I felt as if I had lost not only my sister, but also my parents. I was left alone.

Meanwhile, around my friends, I was a happy 9-year old surf dog and football star. I didn't have any religious instruction and I just blew the whole thing off by saying, "Yeah, Doreen went to heaven and, hey, she's with God. Oh well. So who's my next girlfriend going to be? When's the next baseball game?"

SCENE THREE
McMaster's Park

{1960 - 1965}

5
LIFE IS A
WHOLE SUMMER LONG

When I was six, we moved to Northwest Torrance, a little suburb of the South Bay of Los Angeles, might as well have been Milwaukee, Wisconsin, the setting for *Happy Days*. My mom and dad were the typical parents of the 1950s with a white picket fence framing the yard of their tract home.

Mom smoked cigarettes, drank beer with neighboring housewives, and took care of the kids. Dad worked. The kids went to school and checked in for milk and chocolate chip cookies before making a beeline to McMaster's Park to "Play ball!" It was a churched era that fused religion and the state, "God bless America."

My biggest exposure to religion was going steady with Mary Ann Tierney, the pastor's daughter. But we didn't hang out in her father's Baptist church. We would play Spin the Bottle in the backyard. So I was smooching as a young guy, always going steady with someone: Mary Ann Tierney or Linda Lane or Susie Bowles. I knew all the girls who were available, and they all knew me. God Bless 'em.

I didn't do well in school. I got A's in P.E., but I wasn't interested in other subjects. When school was out, the whole gang went straight to McMaster's Park right behind my house. If you ever saw the movie, *Sandlot Kids* (1993), that was us: "the best buddies in the entire history of the world" playing on "a piece of paradise a half block wide and a whole summer long."

David Michael Walden was Mikey, a happy kid who lived for baseball: hitting homers over the fence and retrieving the balls in the backyard behind left field, carefully avoiding that ominous big dog drooling over baseballs—and *kids*, we feared.

I was competitive and always wanted to be on the winning team. Sports and recreation were so different in my elementary school days. Today the emphasis is on building everyone's self-esteem by eliminating competition—nixing winners and losers—and avoiding any type of injuries. This just leads to a touchy-feely, obese culture that will eventually collapse under the weight of complacency.

Thank God that I still experience the best of the "parties, girls, and surf" from my *Happy Days* era, only it has been rebooted as "hanging out with true friends, loving my wife, and surfing every chance I get."

We ran free in the park and competed in every sport, thanks to parents who volunteered to coach the teams. We threw balls to each other without the fear of getting hurt as a liability issue. Kids bounced off each other then, and they still do today. That's how we learned.

Coaches encouraged kids to do their best, saying, "You can win. You can do better." Sure, not everyone was going to score a touchdown, but one boy would become the best blocker, another the best hiker, and another the best cheerleader.

As an athlete, I had the opportunity to be a natural leader and others always tended to follow me. In football, I was the running back or quarterback who called all the plays.

At the annual awards banquet for McMaster's Park in 1961, the Recreation Director and coaches recognized the "Athlete of the Year." When they called "Mikey Walden" for that honor, my mother stood up in the crowd, yelling, "That's my boy!" I was 11 years old at the time, and very embarrassed. My dad wasn't there. He read science fiction books and didn't engage in my activities. Mom was my #1 fan.

I think the coaches chose me because of one game in particular. During flag football, I was chasing down a guy who had the ball when his foot flew up and tore open my mouth. I was taken out of the game with a bloody face, but at halftime, I begged the coach, "Put me back in the game, coach, put me back in!" He couldn't help but notice that I had heart, so he put me back in the game, and I scored three touchdowns.

6
SHOOTING THE PIER

My life was surfing, sports, and girls. That was it. An incredibly privileged childhood in Paradise, otherwise known as "The Beaches of Southern California": Hermosa Beach, Manhattan Beach, Redondo Beach. "Surfin' is the only life, the only life for me. Now come on pretty baby and surf with me...."

The world was perfect.

As 10-year olds, we'd leave home at 6 a.m. and bike two miles to the beach, pulling our 30-pound longboards—that felt like 100 pounds—on skateboards tied to the back of our bikes. For 15¢, we'd buy hot bread and a 16-ounce RC Cola. That sustained us for a whole day of surfing. We would surf until the afternoon wind died down and the ocean would glass out. Then we'd chase girls and bike home... "Hi, mom!"

In the early 1960s, even before feature films like *Slippery When Wet* were shot in 16 mm, our high school would screen surf films, and it was a big deal. Kids would wait in a long line. Tickets were $1.50—a lot of money then—so we scraped the bottom of the bucket for change. Bruce Brown would get up and narrate live before screening the films he wrote and directed.

The era of Elvis Presley that began in the late 1950s moved to the beaches of southern California where the images of bronzed surfers and blond beauties mesmerized the nation. After the TV sitcom, *Gidget*, starring Sally Field, aired, surfing went national, spreading inland, moving East of the West Coast.

With the Vietnam War in the backdrop along with college students picketing, with riots in the Los Angeles Watts district, as well as Native American protests, what could have been better than making a great escape from all the negativity? But I was still too young for all of that.

The sport was primed for Bruce Brown to give every young-blooded American the ultimate experience: an endless summer. I escaped into it with millions of others, "Let's go surfin' now, everybody's learning how, come on and safari with me...".

I bought my first Greg Noll surfboard in Hermosa Beach from the surf shop across from my high school. Ahhh...the best surf spot was at 22nd Street and Hermosa Boulevard, and the next best was D&W's next to the airport with planes flying overhead—and a perfect break against the rocks.

You were not a surfer until you shot the Manhattan Beach Pier by surfing through the pillars. I probably shot it a hundred times, weaving through the pier, intensely focused so I didn't have to be peeled off the concrete pillars like Gumby—which was never good for the board, either.

I still have a scar from a wipe out contest. We were surfing shore break, dropping in on short waves that crashed almost straight down on the shoreline. We'd run to the nose of our board, and *Slam!* It was all about who could take the scariest wipe out smack into the sand. After one ride, my board flew around and split open my head. I needed seven stitches. But it was radical.

I could show off that scar, which was very cool. I could tell people it was from getting bit by a shark...or by the ball-eating dog at McMaster's Park. (I still have the scar, wanna see?)

SCENE FOUR
HIGH SCHOOL

{1965 - 1970}

7
LITTLE BIG MAN

In my sophomore year of high school, we moved from Torrance to Huntington Beach. I was a 14-year old punk, the new kid at Marina High School so no one paid attention to me.

In P.E. class, the coach was calling students in alphabetical order for the shot put. On class rosters, as a "Walden," I'm usually the last one called. I would use this to my advantage since I have always loved to show off on center stage.

The shot put gridlines indicated various distances from 10' to 40'. The coach stood at 20' because none of the kids could make it any farther. They would take the shot and heave it or throw it without any instruction or style.

I didn't tell the coach that as a freshman I was CIF champion, and I set the record for shot put: 57'. For a little guy, that was big, but it was because I had learned the form and the kick.

I was posing, taking my time, adjusting my fingers around the shot put, squatting down as I flexed my legs, ready to thrust my being into the launch. The kids were mocking me as they watched. The coach told me to hurry up, so I squatted down and reminded myself, *It's all in the wrist.*

Then I just exploded. The 8-pounder went out about 52', over the coach's head and beyond all the grid lines. I was in the club, an instant hero.

8
THE FONZ vs.
RICHIE CUNNINGHAM

Newscasters didn't broadcast fatalities caused by "gangs" because the youth had not yet become murderers, and dealing drugs was unthinkable. Rebels were pretty mild by today's standards: James Darren, the cool surfer who played "Moondoggie" on *Gidget*, or James Dean, a bad dude because he smoked and rode motorcycles. Made in the image of their cult icons, boys were just being boys, and parents didn't worry about where they went or if they stayed out past 9 p.m.

On the sitcom, *Happy Days*, I would have been Richie Cunningham in my letterman's sweater. Fonz would have been played by my older brother, George, a slick greaser who always had his hands on cars and girls.

George was president of the Hodads, a gang who wore black leather jackets, used chains for belts, and drove low riders. The Hodads stood for grease, cars, and racing. They would get drunk and beat people up, especially surfers. The Hodads hated surfers for being weak and pursuing "fun, fun, fun," otherwise known as "parties, girls, and surf."

Surfers wanted to love instead of fight and smoke. The bad of the bad used marijuana. But most of us never touched that stuff or any drugs. We just snuck a beer or mixed sloe gin with Coke. Yuck.

The in-your-face Hodad girls wore low-cut dresses and you knew they were fooling around. On the other hand, the surfer girls were blond and prissy, and I guarantee you that they were just as nasty, but they put on a good front: going to church, but then doing other things in the back seat of woodies (station wagons) at the local drive-in movies. That was where many steamed-up windows could be found…. "Little surfer, little one, make my heart come all undone. Do you love me, do you, surfer girl?"

My brother George showed his true nature in the way he lived with the Hodads. On the other hand, surfers looked like A-students, but were really hypocrites…and I was the biggest hypo-dude.

My dad did not cope well raising me and George, especially George. George took the brunt of dad's anger, and George rebelled—he became a mean guy and was continuously kicked out of school for fighting. This qualified George to be president of the Hodad Club, which meant that none of the Hodads messed with me, his little brother.

All my surf buddies were beaten up all the time, but I made it through high school without having my face trashed. Thank you, George. I love you, man.

9
DON'T PREPARE...
PLAN!

The desire to win came from my Grandpa "Pop" George Walden. Pop and Nana Walden moved to Escondido in the mid-1930s from Indiana. Grandma, whoa, she was a drill sergeant who managed the Women's Department at Sears in Escondido from the 1940s to 1960s. We could always count on Fruit of the Loom underwear for Christmas. Grandma had four children, and scores of grandchildren and great-grandchildren spanning the generations.

Pop was a quiet man of faith and prayer who attended a Methodist church located just off Escondido Boulevard. Like St. Francis of Assisi, rather than speaking words, Grandpa Pop modeled the character of Christ. He lived it out and set an example as a man of integrity who was respected for his involvement with the community. He founded the Humane Society of Escondido and built their rescue center.

Grandpa was a banker who worked for the IRS when it was first founded in the 1930s, so he learned taxes from *the* source. From 1942-85, he owned his own business in Escondido: George Walden Bookkeeping Service. When I was 14 years old, still in high school, he took me under his wing and taught me business ethics centered around income tax law.

Pop would drive me around town, pointing out real estate projects he was working on. He taught me the practical application of business: not simply tax *preparation*, but tax *planning*. There was a big difference because *planning* meant forecasting and looking ahead. He was a visionary.

More than his success or integrity, I was impressed by Grandpa's love. He was approachable. He would hold the grandkids on his lap, and he always had Life Savers in his pocket.

I never heard Grandpa raise his voice but Nana snapped the whip and, boy, you jumped. Grandpa had a way of tuning her way out. She would be commanding orders, and Grandpa didn't even blink, he would keep reading his newspaper and smoking his Tipperellos cigars. Calm in the storm.

My Dad, bless his heart, was a hard worker, but he didn't know how to show love visibly. It was Grandpa Pop who gave me some basic principles of character: follow through, have integrity, and keep your promises. Like Pop.

10
MAKE BUSINESS, NOT WAR

Grandpa showed me how to do things right. During my four years of high school, Grandpa showed me how to succeed honestly in business, teaching me everything he learned in over 40 years at George M. Walden Bookkeeping Service. Grandpa introduced me to commercial real estate and land acquisition.

He taught me how to organize business transactions, how to set up a sole proprietor, a corporation, a partnership, a syndication, a general partnership, and how to file personal and business income taxes. No one who had taxes done by Grandpa was ever audited. What a legacy!

As a 14-year old, I was eating this up. By the age of 18, I had my own income tax practice. Then, before I knew it, I had graduated from high school. It was 1967, and the day after you left school…boom! You were shipped off to Vietnam wearing your letterman's sweater.

But I'm blind in my right eye, which is 20/400 vision, so I didn't qualify for the draft. This was fortunate because I was not a fighter. I was a running back. A peaceful accountant. I liked bugs, and I didn't want to kill anything…or anyone. I was president of a surf club, for heaven's sake.

11
FEELS SO RIGHT,
IT CAN'T BE WRONG

I married the Queen of Job's Daughters whose parents owned a surf, bait, and tackle shop on Huntington Beach Pier. Joy McColister was a beautiful-to-the-max Blond Bombshell, a Surf Queen.

Joy was adopted. She always suspected that she was the child of a love affair from the flamboyant 1950s between a wealthy man from Hollywood and a beautiful young woman. The lovers ran with the jet-setting blue bloods of Laguna Beach, California. As it turns out, she was right.

The late medical giant, Dr. Vincent Carroll, delivered their baby girl in 1951 and called a respected Episcopal couple who had been unable to conceive. Joy became theirs. Scandals in the elite community were heavily-guarded by celebrities attempting to keep their private lives out of the press, so the story didn't get around.

Like her hometown of Laguna Beach that rests on seaside cliffs, Joy is on the edge. She was conceived in a multimillion dollar beachfront cottage, and I cannot remember a time when she did not have a taste for the finest things in life.

Like Stevie Nicks of Fleetwood Mac performing on stage, Joy's presence was completely seductive, and like Helen of Troy, Joy mesmerized men.

When she graduated from high school, Joy flew to Hawaii with her girlfriends. Her parents told me, "Go get her," and

I said, "Okay!" So I boarded an airplane, found Joy, and proposed to her on Waikiki Beach at sunset—the perfect thing for a Surf Dog and Surf Queen to do.

We were married in October 1969. She was 18 and I was 20. Picture us as Frankie Avalon and Annette Funicello in *Beach Blanket Bingo* (1964). Now we were not only living the sitcom *Happy Days*, featuring Joanie and Chachi, but also the classic surfing film set in paradise, *The Endless Summer* (1966).

Although we were good kids, we didn't understand God. Joy was Episcopalian, and I drifted from one church to another—it didn't matter which one. We were married in the Episcopal Church by Father Calley, and Joy was already pregnant. We had made love in Hawaii after becoming engaged.

At the time, abortions were not legal, so Joy and I made a plan. Everyone thought we were going to Mexico City for a romantic honeymoon, but we had arranged to have an abortion there. We had no knowledge, no counselors, and no idea that it was a horrible plan.

The clinic was really a butcher's shop. Joy was taken away from me for three days while I sat alone in our hotel room, absolutely terrified, hoping that Joy would come back to me alive. Who would I call if she didn't? How could I confess, "Mom and dad, I'm in Mexico City and Joy and our unborn baby are dead."

It was stupid to the maximum degree of stupidity. Nobody knew that this precious girl of 18 went through a living hell. It hurts me that it was wrong, and Joy and I suffer for that, but I know my little baby is in heaven. Man, are we sorry, but a God of insatiable mercy forgave us, and not because we deserved it.

Mac and Annie McColister, Joy's parents, were devout Episcopalians and very involved in their church, but more importantly, their lifestyles reflected heaven on earth. When I asked Mac if I could marry his daughter, he said, "Son, are you willing to work hard?"

Mac and Annie worked extra jobs to provide for many widows, giving 12 grandmas in Huntington Beach $15 a week. Mac told me, "Taking care of orphans and widows is practicing pure religion, and this is what you'll do if you're going to be my son-in-law." Annie cut people's hair in her kitchen for extra money, while Mac's day job was working in the oil fields of Huntington Beach.

He was always on the lookout for charitable opportunities, and found the chance to sell firewood, with all the profits going to the 12 grandmas. Mac noticed that construction companies cut the ends off of frames for new houses, and just left the pieces of scrap wood in piles.

Mac thought, "I have a pick-up truck right here. And a friend over there has a sugar company with leftover heavy duty bags that would hold 100 pounds of wood a piece." So Mac talked to the sugar company and got 100 bags, and asked the construction company for the scrap wood.

Once I was married to Joy, I was fair game. Mac recruited me. He said, "You're going to have an extra job, son." I was a strong 20-year old athlete, and along with their adopted son, John, whom I also dearly love, I would stuff 2" x 4" pieces of wood into the bags, and load them into the truck bed 12 bags high. We'd sell each bag to the store for $2, and the customer would buy the firewood for $3.

We sold all the firewood on Beach Boulevard at Ann's Bait & Tackle on the Huntington Beach Pier. Ann's Bait & Tackle was named after—you guessed it—Annie McColister, which meant it was yet another one of the McColister's business ventures that provided for the widows and orphans. I like to think that I had a hand in helping since John and I bagged and hauled all the firewood that was sold for beach BBQs...just so Huntington Beach grandmas could buy their groceries.

There's a biblical principle that says when you visit someone who is sick or in prison, or when you see someone hungry or naked, you see God. There's a story of a Samaritan man lying by the side of the road, having been attacked by robbers. All the church people, whom you'd think would care, saw the poor guy and walked away. They were without excuse.

Once you see suffering, you can't walk by. You have to feed or encourage or clothe the image of God lying on the street.

Mac didn't walk by, and neither did Grandpa Pop who built Escondido's animal shelter to care for stray and abandoned animals. The God of the universe, who is love, says to men like them, "Good job, buddies. You did it to me, man." Amen.

13
THE TOP DOGS'
PROTEGE

I worked for great mentors and ran a consulting business on the side. Soon, I had my own tax, financial planning, and real estate companies. And I tried something new by dabbling in the entertainment industry: I produced a sports series for TV.

In three years, they took off: the tax and financial planning company was doing well, we had extremely profitable leverage in real estate, and the film business was successful. I was a qualified borrower with high credit worthiness and strong projects, so banks offered me loans with a prime rate of interest in the low single digits.

In January 1980, the prime rate hadn't hit its biggest number, 12-14%. Once the banks walloped borrowers with this inflated rate of interest, it was a lender's market in which banks called the shots. This was devastating for housing developers and FHA (Federal Housing Administration) housing costs. We didn't quite see that coming on the horizon.

In the late 1960s, I was hired at Dunn Properties Corporation, the largest industrial and commercial real estate developer in southern California. I had mentors like Lonnie Dunn, chairman of the board; and James Knapp, president and CEO. In his 70s, Mr. Knapp was not only a godly family man and business leader, but also one of the top 100 legal minds in our nation, along with Roger Severson, vice president of finance and a brilliant CFO—and yes, he, too, was another mentor.

I was initially hired as a messenger, and within three months they promoted me to assistant property manager. Soon, I was promoted to assistant secretary to the corporation. There I was: 22 years old with my first business job, wearing a suit, learning big syndications and industrial development, finding investors, scoping out properties in the company helicopter, or flying in John Wayne's old Lear Jet owned by the company.

I learned how to structure a business the practical way: by sitting under very, very sharp people, and combining that with what my Grandpa Pop taught me about taxes.

Most of our clients at Dunn Properties were from Beverly Hills, so I learned how to network with movie stars. We syndicated investors from Hollywood and put together partnerships to buy industrial parks. These were multiplexes plus another 4-5 big buildings which we would lease out as a guarantee to the investor.

I networked with some very top dogs, including one of the biggest law firms in Newport Beach: Kalmbach, DeMarco, Knapp, and Chillingsworth (KDKC). Kalmbach was one of the "bad guys" representing Nixon in the Watergate Scandal who was eventually arrested.

We could ask for a day off when we needed it, but when any of us were ready to put a deal together, we'd work overnight to pull it off. We'd give them 110%.

SCENE FIVE
BUSINESS PLANS

{1970-1975}

14
"BUSINESS DEGREE? I DON'T NEED NO STINKIN' BUSINESS DEGREE!"

I did all this without having to get a degree in Business or Finance. I was a sponge: a good listener, researcher, and an ambitious student in practical—not theoretical—matters.

While I was working full-time for Dunn Properties, I earned my insurance license on the side and became a General Agent, then a Life Insurance and Annuity salesman. Then I earned my Real Estate License and NASD Securities License. Next I bought a tax franchise from an entrepreneur in San Diego, and set it up in Orange County. I paid the owner some bucks, taking it ten steps ahead of where it was.

The San Diego franchise had been a tax service for a client base of teachers. There was a methodology to the franchise, but I expanded our services beyond income tax by adding real estate, syndication, property management, and investments. It became a one-stop shop—and this was in the early 1970s—while the International Association of Financial Planners was being created on paper.

While financial planning was just being formed, I was doing it! I didn't think of it as "innovating" because as a visionary, I saw greater potential in every context. That future became my present reality, and I didn't look back to measure it against the status quo. I'm meant to look out the window as far as I can see for as long as I can see it. There's my job description.

15
THE EXTRA MILE,
A SALESMAN'S DREAM

I had learned to go the extra mile not only at Dunn Properties where I was paid above scale, but also from playing on the varsity football team for Coach Moates at Huntington Beach High School. Coach Moates taught me the winning attitude by expecting more out of his players, saying, "It's easy to throw in the towel, but it takes guts to finish and go the extra mile."

I was a first-string running back. After every practice, we were exhausted, completely toasted, and Coach Moates would say, "You guys can hit the showers," and he would watch to see which players would quit on time, and who would go out and run more bleachers.

Most of the players did hit the showers, but a few of us who went the extra mile and ran another 50 sets of bleachers were first-string. Our team was incredible in 1966-67 and won CIF with the best record since 1911.

I learned a lesson for life on the high school football field, so when I started my own business, I established Coach Moates' principle as the rule. I expected more. I hired the MBAs with the 4.0 and I took care of my people with better wages and benefits. When anyone asked for a break, I gladly approved time off, no problem. But when it was time to put a deal together, my employees gave me extra.

I would assign a task to someone and say, "Don't come back to me unless it's done, because I guarantee you that I will get the job done now...and better—you watch. Don't make me do your job because I'll pick up the phone right now." I didn't lack arrogance or competitive drive.

When I told my workers to rise to the challenge and serve the customer to the best of their ability, they either quit—and some did—or stayed, learned, and grew. That's why the David M. Walden Corporation grew so fast as the holding company and general partner of six sub-corporations: Orange County Tax & Financial Services, real estate, property management, insurance, securities, and motion pictures/TV (4-Way Sports Productions, Inc.).

The client base went from 25 to 3,500 within three years, and we're talking high-quality professionals, including over 2,000 teachers. Our clients were smart and disciplined. They expected us to follow up and to work on schedule. With a solid staff, everything was in order and our clients were well-cared for.

I expected service, and I only hired the best. I surrounded myself with MBA types and people far smarter than myself. I had my in-house CPA and a reputable lawyer. The one thing I had going for me? I was the founder, chairman, and CEO. who controlled the stocks and signed the checks.

Because of our radio ad campaign, clients came to us. My financial planners never had to solicit to get business. People called in and made appointments, so all my staff had to do was sit behind the desk and write applications all day long. It was a salesman's dream.

I gave my salesmen 40-60% of the commission on top of their income. As the owner, I got my cut from each deal, from each of the seven companies.

I was inundated with people who wanted to see me so my

screeners took care of the non-priority callers. To get to me you had to pass through four screeners, moving from the PBX operator, to my secretary, then the assistant secretary, and finally to Ladora Buck, my executive secretary.

Ladora Buck was a character. She loved her Lite Beer and smoked continuously—in the office, car, and restaurants—and she was always eager to drive to Los Angeles in the limo and schmooze with producers. She was in her mid-40s (twice my age) and extremely protective...like a mother. She handled everything, keeping certain people out of the office, toning down my drinking, and loving me like a son.

I can hear her voice to this day as she cheered on my speedway racers to reach the checkered flag at the Orange County Fairgrounds on a Friday night, "Go buddy...Go!" My racers adored their cheerleader.

16
FOREST BURTON,
GENTLEMAN OF GENTLEMEN

Forest Burton was a gentleman's gentleman, and that's putting it mildly.

When I traveled to Los Angeles, I would rent limos from Exquisite Limo, and Forest Burton became my requested driver. After high school, Forest worked the lights at the Golden Bear Nightclub in Huntington Beach where the 22-year old José Feliciano performed as a single act.

José was the first Latin guitarist to make it big in the American market with Bolero songs like "Feliz Navidad" and a reinterpretation of the Doors' "Light My Fire." José went on to record over 45 Gold and Platinum albums and win six Grammies.

Forest served as José's chauffeur for 11 years, until José's second wife got rid of him because she feared that he might break them up by convincing José to toss her off like the first wife.

Forest was interested in a new position and he heard that some movie producer was hiring, so one day Forest showed up on my doorstep. He convinced me to stop throwing away money by renting from Exquisite Limo: "What if you bought your own limo and hired me? You'd end up making money."

I saw it from a business perspective: a chauffer could be my messenger, escort, and host who picked up clients and investors from the airport. And a limo would impress VIPs and enhance our business profile overall. Everybody was a potential client, so I could use the limo to the max.

The limo would become my primary office. I could hold meetings in the limo, where there would be plenty of room to sign contracts. Cellular phones had to be plugged into an outlet in those days and every limo had this feature.

I could get more work done in the limo en route to meetings because I was constantly on the phone, meeting payroll, traveling to sign deals with attorneys...always thinking ahead. My note pad was always in use and ink would be pouring over the page— alas, it was the pre-wireless epoch, so there were no laptops.

Forest offered to work for me full-time if I agreed to buy a limo. It would be a 24/7 job that included washing and vacuuming the car every day, running errands, and escorting clients. Forest didn't have to wear the high, polished black boots and cap. He wore casual dress pants and shirts. And yet he was truly a gentleman's gentleman.

The plan turned out to be flawless. Forest would have my favorite cigar and Heineken ready for me, and that alone made him worth the salary. Other times, he'd run into a restaurant and fill up a Thermos with coffee, then set up a bar in the trunk where he would pour it into glass coffee mugs and add Bailey's Irish Cream from the cooler and serve it to us inside the limo.

Forest took care of the full range of our clients from the world of racing as well as from finance. My secretarial staff would find out what an individual liked and Forest would follow-through 110%.

The richest people would get every item they requested. On the way to the airport in the morning, clients would be treated to their favorite newspaper over coffee, orange juice, and croissants.

Less affluent passengers with simpler demands were also pampered like royalty. Forest would hand a rose to female clients and announce, "Your husband insisted," although it was completely Forest's idea and the husband was clueless.

We would take my two children, Vincie and Jessie (Vincent and Jessica), to school in the limo, listening to Frazer Smith on KLOS FM 102 and rocking out to Rod Stewart: *You're in my heart, you're in my soul. You'll be my breath should I grow old. You are my lover, you're my best friend, you're in my soul....* Then Forest would open the door and let the kids strut into private school, arriving in style.

On a fishing trip to Mazatlan, I caught several big swordfish, but I couldn't take them back on the airplane. I flew Forest and his wife to Mexico for a few days and they drove back home with the swordfish—not in the limo that time, but in a rental car.

One of the wildest rides was vacationing with an influential judge from Riverside Valley where I owned some condos. Forest and I chauffeured him up and down the Strip in Las Vegas, hitting shows and casinos. Since the judge was a boxing fan, I bought front row seats at Caesar's Palace to watch Mohammed Ali's final fight. We spent 10G's ($10,000) that weekend.

17
DRIVEN TO GOD

Even though Forest, like me, had his drug and alcohol addictions, he still told me about his faith in God and his belief that there was something better than pleasure and success. Maybe I didn't always see a difference in his life because he didn't always act like a saint, but I consistently heard things from him that helped.

Forest helped me recognize my weakness for partying so I could leave it behind. He encouraged me to use my strengths: my intelligence, business acumen, and positive thinking. He said I could accomplish anything.

Three years after Forest surrendered to *the* Higher Power in 1975, I switched from being a master of parties to a Master of Theology, applying myself to prayer and reading the Bible daily. After I graduated from Calvary Bible College in 1995 with a BA in Theology, I was ordained and brought on staff with Pastor Brian Newberry of Calvary Chapel in San Diego.

One of my earliest and most memorable pastoral duties was to baptize Forest, his wife, and his daughter. I will never forget the sunny California day in 1998 in the church secretary's backyard where our small gathering stood beside the swimming pool.

Forest's family felt important because I conducted a full ceremony and introduced each of them, explaining how lucky they were to be at peace with God and celebrating the love they felt toward God, one another, and me. Forest's wife, Jane, couldn't swim, and it was the first time she let someone dunk her head under water.

Now Forest drives a FedEx truck, which is a time-sensitive, labor-oriented, and stressful job, so he can't practice all of his etiquette. But he does get weekends off.

18
APPLE PIE
WITH THE CUNNINGHAMS

We attended church on holidays and did everything families living the American Dream would do, like fishing in the Colorado River and traveling to Europe. It was the four of us: Joy, our kids, Vincie and Jessie, and me. We lived in one of twelve custom houses on Crestview Circle in the Villa Park community, an exclusive neighborhood on the tallest mountain in Orange County with a view of the Catalina Islands.

Our home was a 4,500 square foot, southern colonial mansion with a four-car garage and a $6,000 a month house payment. Today it would be worth $5 million. I grew up in a small house with a mom who stayed home to cook and clean. It felt odd to be in a giant villa with a maid.

In the best of our financial years, I provided enough income for Joy to maintain a very nice standard of living to the tune of $18,000 a month. Each of the seven companies sang a small song, but seven small salaries on the same stage formed a chorus!

I wouldn't let Joy get a job. It was her role to work hard as the mom. I wanted her to do her thing—shop or play tennis or go out with the girls. This was the surfer's ultimate dream for his surfer girl.

My typical day looked pretty much the same: up at 6 a.m., play with kids while the maid cooked breakfast, then we would eat together. Forest would pick me up and we would escort the kids to school in the limo.

I would arrive at the office to set up the place at 7:30 a.m. before everyone else arrived. The 4,000 square foot office was decorated by the leading interior designer in Newport Beach with French provincial furniture, and located in a new complex bordering the Disneyland area, with running streams, flowers, overgrown pines, and spectacular views.

When my secretaries arrived, we would have staff meetings, and then it became a very busy day. I would then see my own clients. The managers would run the office, and as the CEO, I had to make sure we were legal.

I spent most of my time with attorneys. By 9:30 a.m., I was out the door heading to meetings with attorneys about legal issues, not law suits. After all, I had 52 limited partnerships to oversee.

I spent three days a week dealing with securities, real estate, motion pictures and distributors in Hollywood. I had the best lunches. By 4 or 5 p.m., I was back in the office, Forest would pick me up in the limo and take me home by 7 p.m. to be with my family.

Joy and my kids were of paramount importance for my well-being. I was chief of Vincie's Indian Guides group, and I was his motorcross coach at the track. As a family, we would spend weekends planted at Lake Havasu doing our number, leaving home as soon as I got off work on Friday and arriving at the Colorado River by 2 a.m. On Saturday and Sunday, we'd fish and boat all day.

Our life story was the epitome of the Beach Boys' song, "Catch a wave and you're sitting on top of the world": "You paddle out turn around and raise, and baby that's all there is to the coastline craze. Just get away from the shady turf, and baby go catch some rays on the sunny surf. And when you catch a wave you'll be sittin' on top of the world." We thought everything was fine, and we couldn't see that there was ever going to be an end to it.

The question is, "When is it going to fall?" Right? The short answer is that we lived in the mansion during the 1970s until the take-down four years later.

19
THE FUTURE OF
TAX PREPARATION

My financial tax planning companies were in the business of thinking several steps ahead. This put us on the cutting edge of the industry.

In the early 1970s, multimillionaires had CPAs and business planners who would forecast their finances for years, but working-class folks went to H&R Block and paid the big bill to Uncle Sam in April. They were advised after-the-fact between January and April 15th—when it was too late to save taxes.

In the 1970s, an income of $30,000-$50,000 per year was solid middle class. No tax advisor went into strategies to save money on taxes or do forecasting for individuals whose incomes were under $50,000. We did.

I told every client—upper- or middle-income—to come in for a free pre-tax planning session as part of our services. We would take the guesswork out of taxes and help clients save money far beyond the cost of our income tax preparation fee.

We did pre-taxes in September so clients would have a good idea by November about what to expect in April. We would look at their paycheck stubs from the previous year to determine their earnings, interest, and itemized deductions.

Then we lined up the numbers with what they had earned in the past ten months, and project what their earnings would be in November and December. This way, we could advise the clients in September about whether to invest in a qualified tax shelter (TSA), or pre-pay certain items for deductions, or start a new business or partnership. That took Orange County Tax & Financial Planning to the next level.

(At this point in my story, I feel as though you've invested in my life. Let's face it, we've become friends, right? So I've consented to disclosing all my secrets—at least for the benefit of left-brained readers—in the Postscript of this book.)

20
THE ENTREPRENEURIAL SPIRIT

As a visionary, I looked beyond and asked how I could work with integrity, offer a good product, use good marketing, and make it work for us and the customer. That's the entrepreneurial spirit.

I was a promoter. I constantly had to look out the window at the horizon, wondering about trends, sales, and the future market…because I had families to feed. As CEO, I was thinking about my staff and their families. I realized that their contributions to the overall scope of DMW & Associates, Inc. was vital.

I didn't take on employees without taking them on long-term, accepting responsibility for their families. For example, if I hired a secretary at $30,000 a year, I would have to generate $200,000 to cover her salary and overhead for three years.

I was motivated to look beyond the present and promote the business in new ways that would bring in revenue. A self-employed CEO has to think this way, otherwise he should work for somebody else.

By the time I made headlines as one of "The Entrepreneurs" in *The Executive of Orange County* magazine, I had the second largest tax and financial planning business in the county. I was proud. I networked throughout the nation, was chauffeured around Hollywood, promoted films, sponsored races, and traveled the world making movie deals.

Now I look at my face in the photograph from *Executive Magazine*, and I don't even recognize the man. He was some naïve young man who didn't understand how others perceived him, and how he understood himself.

Scene Six
Off Road

{1976-1980}

21
THE SPEEDWAY
FUN (FAST!) WORK

What did David the CEO do in his spare time? I multitasked. I couldn't help it. That was my thing: producing, marketing, budgeting, investing…and racing.

Most people toot around on tracks. I never did. I never sat on a motorcycle unless I was going to race. I would race on flat tracks in the high desert of Phelan. I would set up cones, then take out my pliers and strap on my boots and leathers, very tight, and then put on "race face," looking straight-ahead with determination toward the finish line without blinking or emotion. My only thought was, *Do your best and give it your all.*

I raced with Jim Cavanaugh, a business associate from Newport Beach who introduced me to motorcross. Jim and I never just tooted around. From 9 a.m. to 3 p.m., we did nothing but race. We went to win, just like I'd been doing from a young age.

In fact, my son, Vincent, started riding BMX (bicycle motorcross) dirt bikes when he was 6 years old. By the time he was nine, he was racing in the expert class…and winning. As his coach, when he fell off the bike, I made sure he got back on and finished the race. After he crossed the finish line, he could cry.

My coaching didn't hurt him. He learned to put on "race face" even in business, and in 2006 at the age of 32, he is a brilliant CPA and senior manager at a Dallas, Texas, investment firm, Ernst & Young Accountants.

I loved racing on big, oval flat tracks, and I had no fear. I loved the adrenalin rush. There is nothing like coming out of the chute, front wheel kissing the track at over 100 mph. The adrenalin rush just happens because your focus is on getting sideways around the bends. It's all in the upper body strength, body positioning, and strong wrists.

I like to win, so I would hold the throttle wide open with my chin on the tank before instantly straightening up and crossing the handlebars with my front wheel sliding. Holding the throttle just right, I would make the sideways turn, which acted like a brake on the oval track. And boy, you better not hit the "marbles" (loose gravel) because if you did, your front wheel would cross up and pitch you like Sandy Kofax's fastball. You would go flying on your butt.

22
FULL THROTTLE

In the 1970s and 80s, "fun" still involved "promotion," which made sense because I was still a young guy in my 20s and 30s.

As a promoter, I was interested in family-related sports because tax and financial planning was a family issue. I like speed, but horse racing, for example, wasn't family-related, so I didn't buy a racehorse.

I observed that there were large crowds attending auto racing events, so I went to the racetrack to increase our exposure and promote the business. I knew more impressions would result in more business.

Ten years had gone by since the first motorcross film, *On Any Sunday.* The motorcycle industry had outgrown its reputation from the 1970s of either being gang-related, or else conjuring the image of little Malcolm riding over bumps on a backyard track. By 1980, specially-designed motorcross stadiums were built for professionals who raced to the tune of a half a million dollars a year.

And lo and behold, sitting in the bleachers by the tens of thousands were middle-income families who needed to have taxes done, families who bought life insurance and made investments.

Larry Hoffmann was a disc jockey for Los Angeles and Orange County radio stations. His business card read: "Larry Hoffmann, Supermouth." His mile-a-minute, fast-talking style earned him that title. He became my client and then I hired him to advertise my one-stop financial planning shop. In those days, no one other than H&R Block advertised income tax preparation on the TV or radio. Supermouth interviewed me for a radio ad.

We did a mass saturation, blitzing the marketplace to win business, which we called "four-walling" in the 1960s and early 70s film biz. Larry Hoffman was the king of building four towering walls of promotion. I was right there with him. He mentioned OCTS (Orange County Tax Service) all the time, and each time, I became more optimistic. *Oh yeah, there's another plug! This is way cool.*

The company expanded effortlessly and to such an extent that I felt like I was watching OCTS winning a Grand Prix race and I was just kicking back in the grandstands.

Larry Hoffman still announces professional sports and, yes, he's still "Supermouth."

I discovered that one of the most popular sports in Europe was speedway racing, second only to "football" (the game we Yanks call "soccer"). At stadium racing events throughout Europe—in countries like England, Belgium, and Sweden— weekly events drew 80-100,000 fans.

The oval tracks are ¼ mile, just small teacups. The four riders at the starting line mostly ride Jawa motorcycles that have no brakes and run on nitro-methane, going from 0 to 60 in two seconds. When riders shoot out the gate, it's an explosion. The four guys make the turn with no brakes, full throttle, using only the front tire as the brakes. They pitch the bike sideways around the turn, and go full throttle on the straight-aways.

After four laps, the winner progresses to the next level. Four finalists compete in the championship in Europe, racing 16 heats in their leathers for 100,000 fans. It's wild.

I was very selective with the riders and chose only the best to wear my leathers at the Orange County Fairgrounds in front of the thousands and thousands of people who came every Friday night. My racers wore solid bright yellow leathers with giant black letters "OCTS." I wanted everyone to know David Walden's company was sponsoring these world-class athletes.

I paid my riders more and gave them the best equipment, fitted them in the best leathers, and provided them with everything they needed to win the championship. When I needed the extra mile, they would try to set a world record rather than quit. Once again, this was Coach Moates from varsity football—"It's easy to throw in the towel! Go the extra mile!"—and Dunn Properties—"Be excellent!"—in action.

23
OFF ROAD IN CHINA

Orange County Tax & Financial Planning had a very sophisticated client base, through whom I met the Emmy Award-winning independent sports film producer of ABC's Wide World of Sports, Don Shoemaker.

Don and I eventually co-produced the TV series, Weekend World of Sports, a 30-minute weekly show with three, 7-minute segments about people and recreational sports. It was the perfect show for syndication: the film crew would pull into to a family's garage on a weeknight as the guys prepared to race on the weekend. And we'd be at the track, too.

The United States' trade agreement with China broke ground in 1978. Shortly afterwards, at a party in Beverly Hills, I met the Minister of Motion Picture and TV for all of China. Soon I was able to present the Minister with the master reel of Weekend World of Sports, the TV series about everyday people having fun outdoors. It would be the first sports TV series to be marketed and distributed in China.

Don worked closely with Bruce Brown, the creative genius behind the classic surf film, *Endless Summer* (1966), and motorcross film, *On Any Sunday* (1971)—two seminal films that put these sports on the map by connecting them to the lifestyle of the average American family.

On Any Sunday was Bruce Brown's classic motorcross film starring Steve McQueen riding a German motocycle once used by the Nazis. Steve was a visual image of freedom. Reinventing the hardcore, drug-dealing, fight-picking biker image, Bruce created a quirky docu-drama about families having harmless fun on motorcycles...on *every* Sunday. The film reflected Bruce's simple love for safe fun and offered America's heartland a new escape during the tumultuous 1970s.

There I was, sitting with the man who could connect me with Bruce Brown. I knew the potential in front of me and I was going to ride this wave and race this race full throttle. So I asked Don why Bruce had never made a sequel to these blockbusters, especially *On Any Sunday*.

Then I went further and told Don, "Let's call Bruce right now." Sure enough, Bruce's voice came through on my speakerphone and before I knew it, I had an appointment with the man himself.

24
THE ANARCHIST
MEETS THE CEO

Promoting was in my blood and sports gave me a guaranteed adrenalin rush. I produced and promoted TV and film projects through my company, Four Way Sports Productions. So I laid out a plan to purchase the film rights for the first motorcross feature film, *On Any Sunday (OAS)*, from actor Steve McQueen and surf icon Bruce Brown.

It was my plan to capture the ten years of progress since the first *OAS* introduced motorcycles as a fun sport with the help of movie star, Steve McQueen, a time when bikers hopped off 2' curbs in their backyards.

But tooting around in mud puddles and riding over bumps was harmless, simple fun compared to what would happen to the sport over the next ten years.

Families had lined up for the first film and, ten years later, we were certain there would be more kids in line and even bigger profits.

I envisioned filming *On Any Sunday II (OASII)* in a revved-up gear with Hollywood effects. The sport had changed. Megamillion dollar international races would alert the world to a family sport gone ballistic since its conservative origins in *OAS*. *OASII* was a natural, a film that would announce the era of professional motor sports.

Bob "Hurricane" Hannah, the U.S. Supercross Champion and winner of 70 American Motorcycle Association national races, would fly 50-feet into the air at the Los Angeles Coliseum before 100,000 screaming fans. And Kenny Roberts, the five-time world champion, would race on a Grand Prix motorcycle he built. Brad Lackey would be up there, one of the best motocross racers of the 60's, 70's, and 80's, the winner of more championships than any other American. And new heroes like Bruce "The Fox" Penhall, the world champion of speedway in the early 80's, would storm the scene. They would be the four stars of the film, and their stories would become *OASII.*

With ten of my "suities"—my CPA and attorneys—we drove in limos to Don Shoemaker's studios in Dana Point. We sat around a giant boardroom table in his office and waited for Mr. Bruce Brown to arrive.

Bruce was an hour late, and we still waited. Then we looked out the window and saw an old van—an original Ford Falcon box mini-van—that had never been washed. It was painted white, but caked in brown dirt. We couldn't see who was inside.

A man threw open the door. He was blond and wore a white t-shirt with holes (or was there no shirt at all?) and a pair of white, cut-off trousers with stringy ends, no shoes. Right off the ball he challenged us, "Who the f--- is David Walden?"

From my seat at the head of the table, I said, "I am, Bruce." And he said, "F--- this, f--- that. I don't want attorneys or CPAs or anybody else, and you all, including everybody, get out!"

My attorneys said, "You shouldn't be alone with this guy." But I told my attorneys, "You guys split," and I threw them out, or rather, escorted everybody out and then I sat down next to Bruce Brown.

He said, "So I understand you want to buy *On Any Sunday?*" I said, "Yeah, I do." He said, "How much are you willing to pay?" I said $125,000. On top of that, I would be hiring Don Shoemaker's production company for $400,000, followed by the writers and ad agencies.

Bruce said, "F----n Good," and he wrote down the amount on a blank piece of paper. He signed it, I signed it, we shook hands, and then I handed over the first of five installments, a cashier's check for $25,000. I had come prepared and "no" was not an option.

25
OLYMPIC STUFF

My organization sponsored D&J Racing, which stood for Dave and Jim. (Did I mention that Jim Cavanaugh loved beautiful women and racing?) D&J was all about promotion, at first for Orange County Tax & Financial Planning, and then for *On Any Sunday II (OASII)*.

Sponsoring racers brought in business and took our company right up the ladder. Our racers, and our companies, were winners, but only because we were risk-takers. That's what it takes to get the public's attention. My racing stars blew out the doors and kicked butt from the 1970s through the 80s.

For races at Orange County Stadium, I would buy box seats at the starting line. I would hang $100 bills in front of my racers and tell Bruce "The Fox" Penhall, David Simms, Danny "Berzerko" Becker, Bobby "Bugaloo" Schwartz: "Buddies, winning pays big dividends!" Franklin would be dangling in clear view.

My guys knew they couldn't quit. I said, "Don't you let up. It's easy to be a quitter. You get some sleep if you need to, and if you're not eating right, you need to. Take care of yourself. We're representing the United States of America. This is Olympic stuff, for real." (I realize this seems hyperbolic, but my enthusiasm is what it is: full throttle in all things.)

We followed the American team to 44 countries. We shot 400,000 feet of film for our docu-drama, *On Any Sunday II*, "a Bruce Brown classic filled with passion and ambition."

I once drove 1,000 miles clocking 170 mph in my Benz on the Autobahn from Hockenheim, Germany to Imola, Italy, to arrive in time for an interview with the media while promoting my film.

My star, Bruce Penhall, became the World Champion in 1979, the first American to beat the Europeans since 1934. We took four racers to Europe in 1980 and for the first time in history, our American team beat the world teams from England, Belgium, Sweden, Poland, Finland, and Germany.

The crowd went berserk when they saw the cocky American *OASII* racing star, Kenny Roberts, leading the world-class champions on the last lap going 180 mph on his motorcycle.

He popped a wheelie down the finishing straightaway, one hand on the handlebars and the other waving to thousands of cheering Italian, French, German, and a few of us American fans who were all celebrating with red wine and Vienna sausage.

26
JAIME AND HERBIE
RIDE AGAIN

Racing was a fabulous lifestyle. Thousands of families came out to watch the Mint 400 in Las Vegas, the Parker Dam 400, the Baja 500 and Baja 1000...all of the dozen or so race circuits under SCORE (Southern California Off-Road Enterprises) throughout Baja and the Southwest.

My company, Four Way Sports Productions, bought "Herbie the Love Bug" and "modified" him—to put it mildly—painting him bright yellow. I hired the premier VW engine builder for racing in the United States who tweaked the maximum horsepower out of 1600 cc's...and they didn't even blow. He was good, expensive, and worth it.

Every day was spent planning ahead for the 1980 release of *OASII*. We used the racecar and hyped it from 1978-79: "*OASII* is coming in 1980, get ready!" I had "*OASII*" painted all over the sides and roof of the car so helicopters shooting the race would film it, if we were in the lead. My towing vehicle was a motor home with "*OASII*" painted all over it. Hype, hype, hype.

At the Colorado River, I met Jaime Means from the "Means Machine Race Team." Jaime was an off-road racer from Parker, Arizona who had no fear. He had been racing since he was five years old. No one else would ride with him because he was crazy, but so was I. I had no fear and he had the eyes to see desert terrain. Jaime and I partnered up.

We put together three teams of 4-5 people. Each team would carry tires, shocks, and other parts, and spread out along the racecourse, ready to make repairs to get us back up and running...fast!

The key to off-road racing was finishing. Remember, promotion was central for us. Sure racing was fun, but I wasn't interested in racing if I couldn't win. There was no victory in second place. Winning was the deal. That's why we spent the money.

27
GO, BUDDY, GO!

Jaime and I pulled up to the starting line in Herbie and put on race face. With a wave of the checkered flag, we'd speed up to 130 mph through the desert from morning to night. I'd be screaming, "Jaime, you're not driving fast enough! Go, buddy, go, buddy, go!" This moved his adrenalin—which was already over the edge—to the next level.

We were both very, very close to wipe out...and very, very close to winning. Jaime just went faster! *I loved it.*

We're flying over mountains, full throttle, shooting 30-40 feet into the air and it was absolutely radical. We flew down the 10-mile backstretch—a straightaway which was a flat, wide fire road lined with telephone poles—and the car was screaming, our epinephrine, pumping.

There were no windows to break, and we were strapped in with six seatbelts. It was like being in a dragster.

Then Walker Evans, the world-class driver, blasts by us in his 4x4 monster truck with tires 30" wide and a blistering 1,000 horsepower motor is turning 7,000 RPMs at 200 MPH blowing mother earth into our face, throwing back boulders and we were in Herbie the little VW Love Bug and we couldn't let up. We were being pelted—*bam, bam, bam, bam, bam!*

The impact of the boulders, the intensity of the speed, the force of the passing truck—it's the most incredible rush...a thrill. Heaven on earth! Your ribs vibrate from the noise and your heart stops, fear grabs you for an instant but you never—

never!—let off the throttle. Today, there's Fear Factor, but we were living on the edge...and winning. Thank God Walker was in a different class than ol' Herbie.

To win the championships, off-road racers have to compete in many races throughout the year. For many years, Jaime and I finished in the top five, and then in 1981, we finally pulled off the U.S. Championship. Go, buddy, go!

But I never lost sight of the bottom line: my primary role as general partner to maximize the investors' dollars going into the production of *OASII.* The *OASII* racecar was getting plenty of free publicity. Our story ran in numerous sports rags like *Off-Road* and *Cycle Magazine,* which meant free press. Why is NASCAR going off the chart with 15 million people looking at their K-Mart ad? We, too, met our primary goal: *OASII* was everywhere.

The investors in the films didn't realize what I was doing behind the scenes to promote and protect their interests. It wasn't just for fun. My teams wanted to do everything possible to deliver a quality and profitable film on time. (But, let's face it, it was fun work.) Eventually, my investors would come down on me when I was taken to trial.

28
THE GLASS IS HALF FULL
WITH UNLIMITED REFILLS

I was fortunate to remain somewhat outside the inner sanctums of Hollyweird. My office and corporate structures were in Orange County, which was taboo, a No-Man's Land in the mind of Hollywood.

I traveled to Los Angeles a lot as the executive producer and president of Four Way Film Productions, Inc. My job was primarily to cut the deals, so I spent a lot of time with attorneys. I didn't really have contact with the artistic side.

Back in those days, you had to play major league ball. There were only a few independent producers, and yet my independent company was able to produce something the public wanted and that distributors would consider.

I was invited to many parties as a rare breed: an executive producer who actually produced a film that was picked up by a distributor, played for weeks in the United States and in foreign markets, and was nominated for an Oscar for Best Docu-Drama. We didn't win, but it was cool to be selected.

Influential producers who deal in drama are often approached by very attractive, seductive actors—we used to call them "actresses"—so producers could be tempted big time.

Fortunately, I was not involved in drama. I was involved with sports films for TV—docu-drama—and I was mainly dealing with men so temptations were minimized. Thank God I didn't cross over to drama. If I did, I might have gone sideways.

I wasn't a wild partier who downed martini after martini. I liked my wine and enjoyed my Heineken. In my family there is a tendency towards alcoholism, so I have that tendency as well. I enjoy not one, but six.

I was careful not to mix drinking with business, but on trips back from Hollywood after business hours, I let things happen. I was human. Lust of the flesh and pride of life had a hold on me big time. When you are a successful over-achiever and everything is going well, your ego—your pride—goes way up. That's how it was for me.

The limo was an effective business tool, but I confess, there were times when the ladies wanted to be with the producer and his team and we welcomed them with open arms and glasses of champagne. Joy was affected by the limelight as well and had her own fun. We weren't happy. We were desperate to regain control, but we couldn't help heading down the wrong path.

When the experienced surfer looks out at the horizon and sees the giant clean-up set, he starts scratchin', man—paddling as hard and fast as he can hoping that he can make it over the lip. He bursts out the back still scratchin' mid-air because the next wave of the set is even bigger…and he knows he's about to be wiped out.

As an old surfer dude today, I have to hit the 24/7 gyms and lift weights so I have enough upper body strength to stand a chance against those monsters.

29
IT AIN'T SUNDAY

But there's a price you pay, folks, when "the buck stops here." As a leader, I had to stay focused. I had a responsibility to my partners. I was battling the press, trying to run seven companies, and finishing *On Any Sunday II.* As the executive producer, it was my responsibility to deliver on time, under budget, and with the best possibilities for distribution and profit. These were my commitments and goals to the investors from the beginning.

I had signed off complete artistic control as part of the arrangement to retain Don Shoemaker and his production company, DEM, Inc. I was confident that the film would be a success, and I didn't need to be consulted about the content. When we first previewed the film for the press, I was seeing the film for the first time.

I thought I was in the wrong theater. For the soundtrack of the motorcycle film, instead of choosing ZZ-Top, Don used tuxedo music by the London Symphony Orchestra. And the film concluded with USA's hopeful champ, Brad Lackey, losing the championship race, hanging his head in despair, and crying on his wife's shoulder. The End.

The audience is going, *Ughhh.* Now, this film was supposed to be for kids, active families, and the audience from the first *On Any Sunday* a decade earlier. It had to be up, up, up. Audiences can't leave the theater depressed. They would not tell their buddies, "Dude, ya gotta see *OASII,* it's totally rad!" "Bring a hankie" is not a five-star recommendation to a sports film.

The next day, both the *Motorcycle News* as well as *Cycle News* ran the reviews: "*On Any Sunday* it Ain't." I sank from the sunroof in my limo on Sunset Boulevard to the bottom of the cutting room floor. It was trash. *Oh my God, what do we do?*

30
IT'S COMING…
PRETTY SOON

Don would have to redo what was done. If not, I would replace him with a new director and editor. Time was money and time was what I did not have. We had to tell the story in a new way. We had to re-edit the film immediately!

I walked out of one meeting with Don in LA and told him my duty as a general partner was to come through for the investors. But Don would not permit the negative to be cut. Don's attorney called and said, "We own the tonnage, the footage."

Don would sit on our negative—the film—until we proved our case. And this was a problem since the only property that film investors own is the negative. That's all a producer can deliver.

So I immediately hired a horse-power attorney who came recommended by my legal advisors. Mr. James Donovan was a former SEC prosecutor and renowned no-nonsense legal mind. He was 5'4," wore a flat, wide-brimmed hat and horn-rimmed glasses. Mr. Donovan used what is called an Unlawful Detainer, Writ of Possession, Ex-Party approach to right this wrong, and we went to court.

For the hearing, Don's attorney from Hollywood had to appear in an Orange County courtroom because the place of our business was in Orange. Don and his attorney from Hollywood were inconvenienced. That was an insult, but compulsory because he was Ex-Party. I was sitting with my attorneys in court, when Don's attorney storms into the court and screams, "How dare you call me into this court, do you know who I am?"

You don't speak like that to a judge, especially not to an Orange County judge if you're from Hollywierd. That judge stopped the attorney with one word and called the attorneys into the back room. That judge reamed out the attorney to the max.

I had sat in numerous meetings with attorneys, at times in tears, appealing to Don. The court record reflects how many times I pleaded with Don, "You're not doing this to me. You're doing it to the teachers…and to grandmas and grandpas." He was cold as ice. He could care less.

We negotiated with Don…and it didn't take a little bit of money, it took a lot. Don knew we were in a time crunch and that the pre-promotion costs we had already spent would set us back even more because of his lack of cooperation. Our legal team moved as fast as we could in the most prudent way in order to get what was rightfully the investors' property, the *OASII* film negative.

I had no choice but to raise money within our partnership, sell my interests in *OASII* as general partner, and liquidate personal assets to keep the project alive. I was compelled to re-cut the movie. In reflection, I could have stopped and taken the loss. It might have kept me from visiting Chino U!

I raised the money and bought out Don. The can was ours and we were ready to roll. I retained Roger Rydell, a well-known producer, and we took what was *OASII* and re-edited it. We added Boss Scaggs-type rock n' roll music, action, crashes, explosions, and a "riding off into the sunset" with the winning champions.

The second press preview reported, "This is the Bruce Brown *OASII* we wanted and we got it." The movie you see today is kick-butt. It was picked up by a distributor, and if you ask me, it should be a part of every film collection.

Did it make money, who knows? The first *On Any Sunday* grossed $20 million overall. *OASII* could have done that or better. The worst case scenario and conservative market research done before, during, and after the film projected a gross of $10-15 million, but the worst case scenario did not figure in a Mr. B or a Don Shoemaker.

As good as the film is, when you pre-hype from 1978, "It's coming, it's coming, it's coming!" and then it's finally released in 1981 with the first press previews, *"On Any Sunday* It Ain't," the hype loses momentum. We could have recouped the wave within a three-month period, but not after three years.

A motion picture is high-risk. Investors have their write-off and—in the 70s and early 80s—an investment tax credit. But the returning yield didn't reach David M. Walden. It paid for the cost of re-producing the film and distributing it to theaters. It funded a lengthy battle.

SCENE SEVEN
MR. B

{ 1980 - 1983 }

31
OPENING
OR CLOSING NIGHT?
WAS I EVEN THERE?!

A year before the release of *OASII* in the spring of 1981, the bad press was already on me after Mr. B tried to take me down. We had to work hard and fast to keep our sponsors in the loop for promotional purposes.

All the while, I was a player on the field, but only on the defense. The *Orange County Register* was the Raiders trying to keep this San Diego Charger from scoring a touchdown, sending the slanderous linebacker to take me out and take in more newspaper sales. I had to maintain an image, and I had to pay salaries and bills.

The climate I lived in at this time wasn't exactly the most favorable for the film. Even though we lost hype because of the trial and the delay, Roger Rydell and I pressed on. Roger was just the producer and director we needed to pack mega-watts into the film. He got his arms around this jewel and made it work, big time. It lit up the screen!

Perseverance means never, never, never give up. We, the *OASII* team, finished the job and got it distributed. I knew in my heart, *This was a great victory.*

On Any Sunday II premiered during Spring Break of 1981 at the Cinerama Dome on Sunset Boulevard in Hollywood. It was the ultimate dream of an executive producer. Seeing my film on the billboard at this prestigious theater in the heart of

Tinsel Town is pretty hard to top. Kelly Slater, winning the world surfing championship seven times, might have topped it, but not much else.

I cruised Sunset Boulevard riding in the back of my limo, beaming with my wife and kids beside me. In the cool evening breeze, I stood up through the limo's rear sunroof with my son, Vincent, and we couldn't believe the lines wrapped around the block to see our movie.

In front of the Cinerama Dome, six colossal searchlights painted the sky. World champion racers gave autographs in the midst of a giant display of racing bikes.

A colossal motorcross racer shot through space above the crowds lining Sunset Boulevard, flying 40-feet into the air just in front of the brilliantly-lit billboard: *On Any Sunday II*. If you were there you would remember the premiere of *OASII*. I was there!

It's a family film—except the Motion Picture Association gave us a PG-rating. In a scene at the speedway races at the Orange County Fairgrounds with loud engines and screaming fans, my cameraman was shooting the crowds when a guy mooned the camera. So we held the shot and kept it in the film. It's a laugh, but it got us a PG-rating.

Mac McColister, Joy's dad, traveled with me on the movie tour to almost all the motorcross events and speedway races. Mac was semi-retired, and having a blast. Mac designed the *OASII* hats, sunglasses, and lighters in canary yellow with black letters—the happy colors from the Bay City Surf Club.

Mac's son, Jon, was an expert photographer and took all our still photos for posters and action shots for the movie. Jon and I were really close. We went first-class on a couple of the filming shoots and we whooped it up. Hey, I was the executive producer and he was such fun. We were living a fantasy. Very, very sweet!

(It saddens me to remember that Jon died from diabetes in 2002 at the young age of 57. I loved him so much! Jon loved the Lord and he knew someday, I would know God in the same, personal way.)

To this day, I keep my film treasures in the home office I call my "Upper Room" where I am right now as I crank out this section: *OASII* souvenirs like hats and cigarette lighters, a framed *OASII* poster, and an executive producer's chair. The president of a film company and executive producer of a film. Whoa. I did it. And the movie is good.

Seeing my films on TV and in theaters was a satisfying accomplishment, but the high didn't last long. The next day, I had companies to run in addition to keeping real estate developments and film productions rolling. There would be payroll, operating expenses, and more contracts to sign.

Today, I have more joy saying, "Yo, baby, go rent my movie and look for my *Jon* Hancock, 'Executive Producer: David M. Walden.'" It's for you, Jon.

32

A THREAT:
NO MORE SUNDAYS

I was a young, naïve man who did not discern that one of my employees could possibly be discontented. Because I took care of my staff like family, it didn't occur to me that anyone might be resentful.

Often in staff meetings, I would tell my taxmen and accountants, "Guys, if you want to set up your own company, great. You pay the rent, utilities, and salaries. You'll see what I go through, but, bless you, if you want to, go do it."

I would routinely add the disclosure, "Competition is good medicine. The only thing is, you just can't take my clients. They belong to Orange County Tax & Financial Planning."

I continued, "People, I have retained a high-priced radio personality, Larry 'Supermouth' Huffman, to produce, deliver, and place multiple spots with radio stations in Orange and Los Angeles County. These radio spots will promote OCTFS. I will bring in customers for you to service.

"Staff, you do not have to solicit or travel to get clients to buy insurance. Staff, the customers will come to you. They will be lined up every day for you to sell the quality products OCTFS offers. Staff, isn't this every salesperson's dream? You sit at a desk overlooking lakes and trees, while clients are booked for you and you simply write app's all day long."

Everyone smiled. We had happy staff meetings.

We had a file cabinet filled with resumes of candidates

wanting a job with OCTFS. But our turnover was basically zero. Why would anyone want to leave such a good thing? But, then again, a few thousand years back there was this group of guys with Jesus and they had it real good, too, but there was that one who split. Go figure....

I especially trusted my taxman, Mr. B. He was out of work when I first met him. He had formerly worked for the Internal Revenue Service and was experienced in income tax preparation. I had an opening for someone with precisely his credentials, so after he completed the required training and proper licensing, I hired him.

I promoted Mr. B as the tax manager of Orange County Tax & Financial Services, Inc., and trusted him to manage the nearly 3,500 clients and the staff that served them. He became engaged to my wife's best friend and the four of us enjoyed many evenings together of fun and friendship.

It was New Year's of a new tax season and a new decade. When Mr. B came to my house on January 1, 1980, I thought it was a friendly visit. I suspected nothing. Mr. B launched into a sob story, "I'm getting older and I need to stretch my wings." He stayed most of the evening and left about 9 p.m.

I arrived at work earlier than usual the next morning to welcome the team into the new year. As I entered the office, I noticed that Mr. B's office in the far section of the corporate facility was different. I walked at an unusually fast pace and my heart pounded as I drew nearer and nearer. I could feel my blood pressure going higher and higher. *Oh, my God. No way. Can this be so?*

Mr. B had cleared out his office. Keep in mind that in the 1970s, there were no computer databases. Everything was stored on master lists in paper files, and this was "high-tech." It wasn't until the early 80s that computers entered the scene.

Neither was confidentiality an issue. Anyone could pick up a file on anybody else. HIPAA (the privacy provisions of the Health Insurance Portability and Accountability Act passed in 1996) would have had a field day then.

I called Mr. B at home, and sure enough, he was there. He screamed over the receiver, "I'm going to put you out of business! I'm going to take you down!"

I was shocked by this threat from a friend and I asked, "What is the deal? What are you talking about? If you want to compete—fine, fine, fine. I'm there for you. But what do you mean about taking me down?"

Mr. B was firm, "I'm going to put you out of business." And he hung up.

He had already cleared out his office before his visit on New Year's. His sob story was a set-up so I wouldn't suspect anything and he could deceive me on two fronts—at home and in the office. The intentions of the heart cannot be seen by our eyes, but nothing is hidden from the Creator.

I had assigned the VIP case clients to Mr. B, including the editor of the Business section of the *Orange County Register*. The two had become friends. Here was Mr. B, the tax manager of one of the largest companies in Orange County, contacting the newspaper editor with his statement: "I resigned from OCTFS. I left because I thought there might be some funny business going on."

I was about to get a lesson in target practice. Editors take aim at high-profile leaders with their pens. Mr. B's scoop was front-page material for the Business section and I would soon be the poster boy for white-collar criminals.

33
LIGHTS OUT…
THE PANIC

The *Orange County Register's* Business headlines were worded for the greatest effect: "Funny business…something is wrong… tax manager leaves with suspicion…and have yourself a Happy New Year 1980." The newspaper publicized one side of the story: Mr. B's.

He alleged that I was stealing money from teachers and putting it in my own pocket. As a result, the Orange Police Department even called a meeting at an elementary school with teachers who invested in the partnerships. Napoleonic Law was in effect: I was guilty until proven innocent.

I thought, "Wait a minute, those aren't the facts." The truth is that I shared success with the entire staff and Mr. B was well-compensated for his work. But instead of confronting me honestly about his concerns, he began spreading rumors about me. Whether it was greed, suspicion about the way I was running my business, or possibly jealousy over a younger man's prosperity, I did not know why Mr. B was upset.

I was young and naïve to think that I had a happy family and was living *Happy Days*. Suddenly, I regained consciousness on the other side of the TV screen and wondered, "What in the world is going on? Why is this happening?" I had no clue.

I'm not perfect and I know I have made errors. But I did my best to surround myself with the right people. I tried to maintain sales and pay our bills. As the CEO, I couldn't be emotional about this crisis. Although I was angry at Mr. B, I had to stay focused and rely on my attorneys. I still had companies to run…under new and challenging circumstances.

I had no inside connection with the media and therefore, no rebuttal. It dragged on…bad press, bad press, bad press. I was instructed by my legal counsel not to speak to the press because journalists would take my words out of context. So, agreeably, I was sequestered.

When a local, client-based company makes the Business section, everybody hears about it. The switchboard lit up. Clients panicked. My staff didn't believe the rumors, but the press affected our clients so severely that it was impossible for my employees to be productive. Once that happened, I was in a back-peddle stage and behind me was low, low ground…or was it a cliff?

I was given some hope by my attorneys who often reminded me that I would have my day in court. Right. In the meantime, time was taking its toll. I was being wiped out. In the meantime, Mr. B had my files.

A year and a half after the *Orange County Register* headlines announced Mr. B's reasons for leaving, a newly-promoted officer of the Orange County Police Department Fraud Division was given the assignment to investigate me.

The fraud investigator felt he had enough evidence to get a search warrant. I thought a search warrant only granted permission for a specific purpose, such as, "You may take X." Although we had nothing to hide, my secretaries were met by three policemen bearing arms who took all the files and checkbooks—more than they were supposed to. By the time the police returned the files, they had copied everything and felt they could put a case together.

34
CUFFED TO A GURNEY

My net worth was almost $3 million in 1980, according to my audited statement. But as the media's smear campaign moved across the land, it sort of bulldozed that "net worth" in a hurry. I would have to prove my innocence in a trial that was coming down the pipeline.

I tried to stay calm by repeating my position, "I'm innocent. Our documents and records will prove that when we have our day in court. This is America and this is a just court system. Grandpa Pop taught me that and I still believe it today. The system is not perfect, because perfect is not of this world. But we'll do our best."

But I became impatient with all the waiting and wanted to take action: *What should I do? I know I'm not the only one in the world who has suffered like this. There must be a way out.*

Clients were leaving left and right. At our peak in 1980, we had 3,500 clients. By 1983, we had 500. My assets were quickly being liquidated so I could pay for legal expenses and salaries. We downsized, moving out of our large office and laying off people to get ourselves in a position of defense.

I was dealing with film crews in Europe and we had challenges in film production. I had real estate expenses out there with a prime rate of 15-20%. I couldn't sell my property in Beaumont, and I was making land loan payments of almost $10,000 a month between 1979 and 1982—almost $225,000!

It didn't help when an ex-football player at a real estate investment company misrepresented my client, leaving me to repay my client the $10,000 he lost. When I learned the company was all a fraud and threatened to turn him in, he started wailing on me, damaging my kidneys and putting me in the Emergency Room.

By then, the investigating officer felt he had enough evidence of fraud to charge me with grand theft. In those days, a mere $400 discrepancy constituted grand theft. In the officer's observation, more than this amount was unaccounted for. In fact, he alleged that millions of dollars had been embezzled from teachers and put into my own pocket.

The judge ordered me to be arrested. The Orange County Police Department's Fraud Investigator and his deputies arrested me while I was lying on a gurney in the ER of Orange County's Hoag Hospital. Surprise!

The arresting officer read my Miranda Rights and within a few minutes, news crews shoved their way into position and cameras flashed. Now I was some kind of notorious celebrity. I was "delicately" put in the back of the patrol car and whisked away to the medical ward at Orange County Jail.

Sitting in the back of the police car with officers carrying shotguns on both sides of me, I thought, *Mr. B really didn't come to my house. I'm not really here. This must be a nightmare—what else could it be? I don't have a clue what jail's like. I've never been near one. Give me a break, I'm a surf dog from Huntington Beach.*

I think I was under a little stress.

35
THIS'LL BE THE DAY
THAT I DIE

On February 3, 1983, David Michael Walden was on every major network station: CBS, ABC, and NBC. "Orange County Tax & Financial Services, David M. Walden allegedly embezzled millions of dollars from teachers...." "Movie producer...." "White-collar criminal...." "One million dollar bond...."

I watched the news from the medical ward in Orange County Jail. My wife saw me. Everyone saw me.

I stayed with 90 men in a packed 50' x 30' cell, sleeping under the corner of a table. When the judge realized I had no "priors" (no record) and that I had every intention of proving my case, he said, "You're out on your own recognizance. See you back in court for a week-long preliminary trial."

Three days later, I was released. I walked down the ice cold, 150-foot concrete hall from my damp dungeon toward the exit thinking, *I'm facing a trial and every station on TV has already decided that I'm guilty.* And I was believing it, imagining that I had done something wrong, thinking I was a bad guy and wondering, *Why am I here? Why would somebody accuse me of doing something I didn't do?*

I was a mental case. All I heard was, *You're no good. No good. Worthless.* Negative, negative, negative. That was hitting bottom.

I traipsed down that long corridor out of hell and into purgatory. The real estate market was wiping out, the ordeal with the film exhausted my last hope, and my family was in pieces. The future was heading over-the-falls of a 50-foot swell and that is definitely a total wipe out. I know what it means to be steamrolled, folks!

On February 5, 1983, I walked out of Orange County Jail three days after my arrest, released on OR (my Own Recognizance) and went home to wipe out of this life. *Gee, this was all for nothing*, I thought, *I might as well check out*. Yes, I was going to kill myself.

It had been a tough 18 months, so I bit the bullet and liquidated. Because we had been threatened by investors, my brother-in-law, Jon, let me keep his 357 Magnum. He wanted to protect his sister, Joy, and me. I never owned a gun in my life.

At home, I took Jon's 357 Magnum and a six-pack of Coors Lights into the backyard. I packed down the beer in thirty. All around my head were negative voices cursing me. I cocked the gun, and I had my finger on the trigger. I accepted the reality that I was gone.

I held the gun to my head and just as I was about to squeeze the trigger and pass into utter darkness—forever—an audible voice from nowhere spoke to me, *I love you, Mikey*. The bullet should have been traveling along the barrel by now, but it was stopped. The words penetrated me instead.

The voice was so bizarre, so different. It came from another realm and was so far removed from what I had been hearing, it caused a complete paradigm shift. I had been overwhelmed with destructive thoughts and fearful images of no hope and no future. Out of all of this dread, at the 11th hour, came love.

Nobody was around. I was alone in my backyard and I heard an audible voice. It was talking to Mikey, surfer Mikey, my inner man…the little guy who played Spin the Bottle with Mary Ann

Tierney. I had no choice, no option, but to respond.

If that voice had not entered into that moment, into that iota of time, if it had come just a nanosecond later, I would be dead. I know that I know that to this moment, every breath I take today—I mean this with every fiber of my being—every time I walk, it is an extra bonus. It is a privilege to be alive.

If that voice of love had not intervened. . . .

I love you, put the gun down. I believe it was God.

Now it makes me think of the story from the Bible about Stephen who looked up and saw a visible Jesus just before he was about to die. I could say that Jesus stood in my place and took my bullet so it was never fired.

Now where was Mikey?

36
JOHN 3:16

The only thing I knew was to go to the Bible. As a 5-year old, I went to Sunday School at First Baptist Church where we sang, "Jesus loves me this I know, for the Bible tells me so." I had gone steady with Mary Ann Tierney, the pastor's daughter. That was the extent of my theology.

So when I heard the voice prompt me, "Go to the Bible," I had no idea where to turn. I hadn't looked at the Bible in 20 years.

I put down the gun and dusted off the Bible. The only thing I knew about "the Bible telling me so" was from watching football games on TV. I remembered seeing the signs, "John 3:16." I thank God for those people holding up signs at ball games!

I found the Gospel of John, "For God so loved the world that he gave his only begotten son, that whosoever believeth in him shall not perish but have everlasting life." I didn't want to perish. I read, "You shall not perish." I thought, *Bingo.* "Will have everlasting life."

Suddenly life looked good to me because I should have been dead. Now I'm walking around supernaturally. I thought, *Love—that's different...and weird.* I didn't understand it, but I bought it.

In my spirit, in my inner man, I said, *Okay, what do you want me to do?* Rather than hearing an audible answer I listened with my heart and sensed the reply, *You probably ought to read it.*

The mental cacophony started to play in tune as I was being prepared internally. That voice gave me confidence and hope…and a future. I was ready to face a trial where it was me and a loving God against the State of California, the Department of Corporations, the Securities and Exchange Commission, the District Attorney, the Police Department, and Mr. B's Fan Club bringing their case down on one newly-empowered "Mikey"…me.

The whole stage was set. It was ready for lights, camera, action. Take your places Prosecutors—the County of Orange and the Department of Justice—and the Defendant—Mikey. Let the trial begin. The DA wanted to put me in jail for 12-20 years. The screenwriters for the Prosecution had already written that tragic ending. My version was considerably different.

Was it going to be Don Shoemaker's losing version of *OASII* with Brad Lackey hanging his head in defeat, or my revised *OASII* with the good guys riding into the desert sunset?

I told myself, *I want to be slow to speak and quick to listen. I will not let myself get tweaked. I'll go back to my business training and remember my coaches and mentors who told me to focus, not to quit or throw in the towel, but to play hard, with integrity, keeping my promises. Finishing is winning.*

The negative thoughts were extinguished once I stopped feeding the blaze. Now I had to replace the lies with the truth: *No, I'm not guilty! What is this "lie" crap? I need truth from somewhere, so where do I turn? I'll read the Bible and live by its lessons, but I don't know theology so I'll need something practical, just the basic stuff.*

I found Proverbs, "Be wise, quick to listen, slow to speak." James, "Be doers of the Word not only hearers." I thought,

This sounds simple enough. I can do that.

After having 52 limited partnerships and overseeing seven corporations, I wanted to die. Here was my chance at rebirth. If I was going to live, my life had to change.

There was no way I could cure myself. I needed a physician and on February 5, 1983, at 11:30 a.m., the Great Physician made a house call. The "me virus" was cured by "God's love vaccine," and I began to see others as more important than myself.

PART
TWO

CHAPPY

Scene Eight
The 90-Day Trial

{Spring/Summer 1984}

37
TAKING A STAND

At 11:30 a.m. on February 5, 1983, I died. At 11:31, I was a new person with a whole new outlook that said, "I'm going to be doing it the way you teach me to do it, God. This is varsity, and I'm first-string, a world champion who has done it before and will do it again. I'm going to fight...fight...*FIGHT!*"

I liquidated all my assets so I could pay the attorneys' fees. I had mouths to feed, so right in the middle of the pre-trial—as my corporations were forced to become inactive—I had to take a job. I worked for a mortgage consultant in Santa Ana. I was even voted "Man of the Year" in my first year with this firm. I keep the plaque in my "Upper Room" as a reminder that even in adversity, God still prevails through a broken man.

I was back on track and ready to fight with wisdom, common sense, and truth. Even as the Defendant, I was ready to go after the Prosecution. I entered the battlefield with my defense attorneys and every day after work, for over a year, I rushed to spend 4-8 hours a day literally living in Todd Landgren's Santa Ana office. We began reviewing every piece of paper from the past ten years, looking at every contract, document, and thousands of checks, one-by-one.

I was charged on six counts: (1) fraud, (2) embezzlement, (3) and (4) two counts of grand theft, and (5) and (6) two counts of Corporations Code Violations under SEC 25102. If found guilty, I could have been sentenced to more than 12 years in prison.

I was so wrapped up in events that every phone call, every letter, and every visitor put me in a defensive position. A psychologist might have said I needed some serious therapy because I know some serious paranoia set in ever since Mr. B's accusation of January 1980. Therefore, starting February 5, 1983, at 11:31 a.m., I pro-actively conditioned myself— one day at a time, one year at a time—to defend, defend, defend....

It has taken me over ten years not to have to defend who I am, and to be able to answer the phone without any suspicion. The mind is a powerful thing. Put in trash and you get polluted brain cells.

The trial was scheduled for March 1984 in the Superior Court of Orange County. Next door to my courtroom, a dentist was on trial for administering overdoses of medication that resulted in the death of a patient. That made big news.

Then there was David M. Walden, Weekend World Partnership, Orange County Tax & Financial Planning, white-collar criminal, in the auditorium with TV reporters, the DA's team, the jury, and the crowd.

I arrived 1 ½ hours early, parked a few miles from the courthouse, opened the Bible to the practical books of wisdom—ol' James and John and Proverbs—and then power-walked to mentally prepare myself. I would pray for help with each step, "Give me guidance, give me guidance, give me guidance."

Inside the courtroom, I would set my briefcase on the table and lay the day's files in proper order alongside a small Bible. That Bible, my *Hope Instruction Manual for the Future*, stayed open right in front of me every day of the trial.

Todd Landgren was one of the best trial lawyers in Orange County, a brilliant scholar in law and securities. He was a perfectionist, putting me through drills on every detail of my operations so we had all the facts and there would be no surprises. Instead of taking a more profitable, short-term case, Todd devoted his time to mine because in his heart, he knew my intentions were honorable.

There is a big difference between people who are visionary leaders and people who are managers. A manager does it the right *way*, whereas a visionary does the right *thing*. I was a visionary. I am a visionary, so I do the right thing. I might not exactly do it the right way, fine. But I get it done, even if I have to go around this way and use these—legal—channels to do it. I can't help what I am. This is what I'm made of.

As an entrepreneur with a vision, my intent had been to provide my customers, my staff, and their families a professional organization that promoted integrity and quality products, services, and results. I believed this concept and its implementation would result in solid growth and prosperity, so everyone involved would benefit. It was never my intent to violate the State or Federal law, let alone the ancient Supreme Law ol' Moses brought back from the mountain. Steal... from teachers?!

Having over 3,000 clients, 52 partnerships, and seven currently registered California corporations meant a lot of bookkeeping by my loyal and gifted staff. And it meant federal, state, and local agencies were looking at us all the time.

For a small organization with a lot of business, OCTFS did an excellent job with the combined talent of dedicated professionals licensed in securities, insurance, real estate, and accounting. Was it perfect? No. What's perfect?

Maybe I went too far in trying to preserve the customers' interests in the challenges with Mr. Shoemaker in re-editing *On Any Sunday II* ? Maybe I relied too heavily on the advice of attorneys, CPAs, and MBAs regarding the film and real estate partnerships?

Of course I made mistakes, but my intent was always to further profits, to protect our clients' interests and in doing so, I wanted to do the right thing.

Who in this world is the guilty one? The answer: the one who throws the first stone.

38
THE VERDICT

Monday through Friday from 8:30 a.m. to 4:00 p.m. throughout March, April, May, and June 1984, hundreds of witnesses were called and 7,000 pages of transcripts were written. One day of a jury trial is a long time...mine lasted 90.

There was an incredible amount of documentation, especially regarding how the money was circulated. I was questioned on the stand for days and made to identify every check.

Ultimately, there was no missing money. In fact, the CPAs from the Orange County District Attorney's office and the State of California Corporations Office audited my books, and reported that I was owed $142,000 and some change in fees, commissions that I refunded back to the partnerships and loans I made to the companies.

Often, although I was entitled to a management fee as the acting general partner, I deferred the compensation and chose to defer it back to the deal. I didn't need the fee and the profit helped the company make even more profits. It was good business to keep the customer happy by lowering the costs of doing business. It worked well.

When the jury heard I was owed money, the District Attorney made the CPAs audit the books again. A week later, the CPAs came back with the same amount. David Walden is owed $142K according to our audit. That's right: exactly $142,550, Mr. B and Mr. *Orange County Register* Business Editor.

June 1984. The jury ruled on the four counts of fraud, embezzlement, and grand theft. But the jurors did not rule on the two counts of violation of the securities registration, California Corporation Code Section 25102 (CCC-25102). The issue dealt with the way my attorneys drafted the limited partnerships in the beginning (1978-79). In particular, the Weekend World 1-50 offering (*On Any Sunday II* and the TV series Weekend World) and a certain real estate offering which was a $1.2 million medical building I purchased in 1980 utilizing a private placement partnership offering.

The judge would rule on these counts because they were technicalities of the law.

So, the jury returned and they unanimously ruled "not guilty" on three counts, and hung on one count of grand theft (ten for "not guilty" and two for "guilty"). The one count that was hung was not challenged by the DA and therefore I was not charged with the crime.

There I was: not guilty on four charges of fraud, embezzlement, and grand theft, but guilty on two counts of violating CCC-25102. Since I was cleared of the serious crimes and there was no missing money, based on prior verdicts, the worst we imagined was a fine and either a suspension or restriction of my licenses for up to three years.

Everybody won on that trial, except one party. The movie was made and distributed. We sold partnerships and properties and the real estate investors made a double-digit profit. All the attorneys were paid…a lot. The only one who didn't win was "The System": the District Attorney, the State, the County, the City of Orange and us, the taxpayers.

Don't worry about what I got. At the end of the day, I got to leave court without handcuffs. I was ready to rebuild my life. The accusations were silenced and I had my wife, kids, home, and I was ready to kick butt in business.

Four years of humiliation, bad press, search warrants, legal preparation, and preliminary trials boiled down to the Superior Court trial of David M. Walden versus the State of California. My 90-day trial ended on June 2, 1984.

After the trial, I asked a few of the jury members about the two dissenting votes. I was told the two "guilty" voters simply thought that with all the business OCTFS conducted, I had to have been off by $400 somewhere along the line. Essentially, they felt any successful entrepreneur would realistically be guilty of grand theft.

I couldn't tell you to this day if a technical violation actually did occur. If so, there was a form of misrepresentation. I relied on my counsel. They were all highly experienced and respected professionals. When they testified on the stand, they stood behind what they had prepared for me. I am so glad I live in America. The System works because we do have freedom of speech and wonderful rights.

The trial was over. I was broke—wiped out—but I provided the defense. The jury concluded that what Mr. B alleged was not true which meant that I wouldn't be spending the next 12 years in a cell. Whoa, yes, that was victory!

But ultimately, the real trial ended on February 5, 1983, when love—real love—entered my life. That was the ultimate "not guilty." There was no doubt: I knew that I should be dead, but instead, I had the experience of a new hope.

39
IN THE ATTORNEY'S
LOCKER ROOM

If you want the official legal-ese for the charge, you can wade through this chapter. Legally, film and TV offerings were limited to ten partners per offering. All investors were related to my tax and financial company either as a client, family member, or friend of the client. Each partnership owned a TV series and an interest in a motion picture, *OASII.*

In the real estate offering, I had a tenant in common with limited partners who owned the property. In the Prosecutor's opinion, this constituted fraud, embezzlement, grand theft, as well as misrepresentation in the language of both offerings.

The counsel I received as the general partner and the representations to the investors was that the private placement status was just that, a *private* offering, and not a *public* offering. Therefore, the partnership was not a violation of CCC-25102.

For the record: the tenant in common made a very nice profit, the tenant's attorney made a sizable legal fee, and when the property in the affluent area of Pasadena was sold, all the limited partners made a nice profit, too. This was the 1980's version of living *Happy Days.*

The attorneys who prepared the offering even communicated with the SEC for confirmation. After a thorough examination of the rules, my legal team determined that even though our private offering involved investors from our own client base, it didn't need to be registered with SEC. My attorneys were certain that the movie was not a public offering and therefore exempt.

The judge ruled against me. His opinion was that on the two counts involving Weekend World and the medical building, I was guilty of a "general intent" crime (an "oops") and not a premeditated specific intent crime (a "gotcha"). Nonetheless, guilty!

SCENE NINE
Oops!

{Fall/Winter 1984}

40
SENTENCING

After the "not guilty" verdict on June 2, 1984, I expected to be congratulated. After 90 days of intense testimony and over 7,000 pages of court reporter transcripts, I was waiting for the bailiff to say, "See ya. Get lost. Next...."

Then two short months later in July, I get a call from Todd Landgren, my trial lawyer, and he said, "Sit down. I've got to tell you two things. Good news and bad news. Good news is you get a bottom bunk and a Captain's clerk job."

What are you talking about? I thought. My attorney's voice lowered to a shade of gray as he said, "The bad news is that you will have to serve time in state prison." *Me...a man who was found "not guilty"?*

Todd continued, "Look, 'The System' spent more than a million on the investigation and the 90-day Superior Court trial. If the judges don't get some time out of you, heads are gonna roll. Therefore, you've *got* to go to prison."

"Let me see if I have this straight," I told Todd, "*I* am going to go to prison? I *am* going to go to prison? I am going to go to *prison* for an 'oops'? A general intent CCC violation?"

Todd said, "Yes. And your hearing is on October 12th, so you'll need to get your house in order." *Not sweet.*

I was in total shock. So The System wasn't the only loser. The trial had just ended and suddenly I had three months to get my house in order before I would be packed off to the joint like some mobster.

I had no money and I didn't want to borrow money to post a bail. I told my family, "This is a setback. I understand 'The System.' If The System wants to take you down, it takes you down. Who am I? Can a little guy like me fight City Hall? I had better just cooperate. First and foremost, I will take care of my family. I'll get our house in order, and then I'll go to jail. We have aunts and uncles in the neighborhood who can help, so let's ask the family to come together while I do my time.

"I know enough law and have access to the prison library. I can have a court-appointed attorney assigned to me and appeal the ruling to the 4th District Court of Appeals. Things will be okay."

Things were not okay! I became a foreigner wandering in the wilderness. Life seemed so alien to me.

At the follow-up hearing on October 12th at 9:00 a.m. in the Superior Court of Orange County, I stood before Judge Thompson for sentencing and this time, my hands were not shackled. I was well-dressed, wearing a suit.

Judge Thompson read the jury's verdict, "The jury finds the defendant not guilty on the four counts of fraud, embezzlement, and grand theft." He continued, "However, in my opinion, on the counts relating to the technical violation of the Corporation Code 25102, I find the defendant guilty.

In the opinion of the Judge, I was guilty of what is known as a "general intent crime," an "oops." I was president and even though I relied upon legal counsel, I should have known the law.

The documents my attorneys prepared for the investment partnership in question involved a "private placement" and not a "public offering." So the attorneys erred. There was no fraud, no missing money, but the judge ruled that the technicality was broken: "I sentence you to the minimum: 16 months in Chino State Prison."

Judge Thompson wrote up the two felony counts and reduced them to one technical misdemeanor. Basically, he gave me a speeding ticket.

But all I heard was: *Do not pass "Go." In fact, pay the State all you have until you're wiped out.*

Slam! Down came the gavel.

Then Judge Thompson consoled me with a mysterious promise: "David we will make it go smoothly for you." *How could he make my life go smoothly for me outside of the courtroom...once I left his domain?*

The guards clipped my wrists tight with handcuffs and escorted me out of the courtroom.

41
MAN TO MAN

I was sentenced to Chino on October 12, 1984.

Shackled, naked, hosed down, screamed at, humiliated. There is no way to describe this. I know our precious Jewish friends had relatives in Auschwitz who were reduced to the most basic levels of inhumanity. My experience was nothing in comparison, but I had a little taste of what they must have experienced.

I soon discovered what the Judge Thompson's mysterious promise meant: when I got to Chino State Prison, I would be moved quickly through The System. I would get the best job and my bunk would have the best view. In other words, somebody at the courthouse would call the Captain at Chino State Prison and say, "Go easy on Walden. We owe him."

I got the best bunk in the whole prison, and you don't just *get* the best bunk. You have to earn it. I landed in the bottom bunk with a view of the Anaheim Hills. The cell was about 4' wide and 8' long with a cabinet, two bunk beds, and a little toilet. I displaced the guy above me who had been in Chino for years, and still had not gotten the privileged bottom bunk.

He was a buffed-out, 38-year old who was in and out of prison his entire life and spent his time lifting weights. And he didn't like me for the simple fact that I had the bottom bunk. He said, "Man, I don't know how you pulled that one off."

My every thought was on how to survive. Because I maintained my first-string running back physique and could still bench-press 300 pounds, he didn't mess with me. I wasn't aggressive or large, but my upper body was strong. Every time I walked into the cell, I would just stick out my chest and grunt as I sauntered my "don't mess with me" strut. Fortunately, he didn't mess with me—that mean guy could have ripped my face off.

Another aspect of my royal treatment was the gift of a job in the clerk's office working for the Captain of the Guards. I would wake up at 5:30 a.m. with the rest of the prisoners, and work until 10 p.m., much later than the other prisoners. But I imagined it was as close as a hostage could come to enjoying a vacation.

For meals, the other prisoners had 30 minutes to wait in line, get their food, and eat. They would usually be served large bowls of beans and rice, or freeze-dried chicken from 1950 that had turned black from freezer burn. Everyone looked forward to tacos once a week. Not me. Every day, I ate eggs and bacon for breakfast, and hamburgers and chicken for lunch and dinner.

Directly outside my office door was freedom. I sat in front of a typewriter and I would type up job assignments for the inmates on 1" x 8" slips of paper and deliver them to the men in their cells. Sometimes, jobs would be changed, effective immediately. Unfortunately, I had no influence over who got which job.

Because I had time on my hands, I wrote a few screenplays. *F.M. Story* was about Frazer Smith, the top DJ in Los Angeles during the 1970s and 80s. From 1977-82, my kids and I would listen to him as we cruised in the limousine along Pacific Coast Highway.

The historical professor/inventor at Columbia University who discovered the FM frequency in the early 1920s was set up by corporate media, and ultimately took the plunge from a 30-

story high rise in Chicago. My screenplay opens at the instant the inventor, Edwin Armstrong, hits the ground. The scene cuts from the black pavement to the bright white maternity ward where a newborn boy screams out life as one life ends— the inventor comes back to life as America's future DJ, Frazer Smith, who restores the inventor's legacy. Sitting at my clerk's desk, I could relate to both men: the disillusioned inventor, and the spokesman for justice.

The second screenplay was called *Catch Me* about a mobster boss I met at Chino. His true story was larger-than-life and had the potential to be picked up by a producer whom I knew from my Hollywood connections. This was a funny and moving story about the mob being one step ahead of a Peter Sellers-type inspector…with phony banks and funny papers and millions coming in.

The kingpin was finally busted with over $35 million in his motel room. He was using $100 bills as fuel to cook his hotdogs. Dogs and Franklins on the BBQ.

I wonder if I'll ever do anything with the screenplays.

42
JOY'S DIVORCE

Joy saw that the plug had been pulled. She was no longer the successful, materialistic Surf Queen, wife and mother after losing her big, beautiful home, her Mercedes-Benz, her assets, and her cash in the bank...everything except her looks and children. I feel that I was guilty of putting her on top of a pedestal and then removing it so she fell. And now she had to answer the question, "What does your husband do?"

From the time the *Orange County Register* reported the story in early 1980, her friends began to ostracize her and she finally started caving in. The trial alone would result in post-traumatic shock.

Joy was going through hell, believing in my innocence and defending me, but after four years, it got old. She started to question my innocence, "Is it true...did you really steal the money?"

Because I had a transformational experience in February of '83, I acted differently, and I talked a lot about God.

A hard lesson I learned was that "perfect" doesn't last. It gets eaten by moths and rust.

Joy didn't have this transformation so she couldn't understand my new sense of peace and self-assurance, nor all of my references to God. She didn't know me. She thought I went over the edge and said I acted abnormal and spacey.

On the other hand, I felt as though I had found a sense of purpose: applying wisdom in order to have a successful life, which I no longer defined as "cruising Easy Street in a limo," but as "steadily plodding down the right path." Joy thought I should be worried, but instead, I had a new hope, a goal, and the integrity to follow through.

43
CHRISTMAS
IN CHINO

As difficult as it was, I had been married to Joy for 15 years, and we were still a family—at least that's what I thought from my vantage point behind 30-foot walls topped with barbed wire. Through the trial and during my prison term, I was relieved that my family had the support of both of our parents.

On December 15, 1984, I was ecstatic when I heard my name over the broadcast system, "David Walden, go to the visiting area."

My heart raced as I sped to see my wife and children just a moment away. We all hugged, but I felt a chill. Even when Jessie and Vincie handed me presents, my kids felt numb. Then Joy invited me to take a walk with her around the yard.

She had graduated from bartending school and began tending bar, when along came a rich man who told her, "I'll take care of you." Joy confessed to me, "I have to make a choice between you and him." And she chose him.

Above every detail of the trial—every argument with Mr. B or the *OASII* director, Don Shoemaker, or being on the witness stand for 90 days—Joy's good-bye was the hardest blow. We had been at odds, but with a divorce, the whole world would cave in. I was buried a million times.

From that moment on, I lamented. She was my high school sweetheart, my buddy, my Little Surfer Girl. We were Mikey and Joy. I had proposed to her on Waikiki and we had an abortion together. We loved our children, but my best friend took my children, my life. She took my arms and my legs and left me with a stump, and she didn't take my head—bummer—because then I would have died.

The only way for me to heal was to sit with the deep, guttural sadness and wail in grief—or rather, lament—until its season passed. This lasted two weeks, all the way until Christmas when I was relieved of the pain. It's a given: comfort is for those who mourn. *The Message* says: "You're blessed when you feel you've lost what is most dear to you. Only then can you be embraced by the One most dear to you."

Joy wanted a fast divorce, and I signed off.

44
TWO FRIENDS,
CLOSER THAN BROTHERS

From my bunk, I could hear the old 91-Freeway to Anaheim and Riverside. It's not natural for humans to be caged—it has a permanent, psychological effect. There's no way to describe what it's like unless you've been there.

Friends, relatives, everybody bailed. Apart from my dad, my brother, Jimmy, and my cousin, Brad Stoddard, only a few wonderful people came to see "one of the least of these," one of the lowest of the low: this inmate quarantined from society. My neighbors, Brian and Donna Elliot, made sacrifices to see me, and two special friends, Stephen Bruce and Richard Mills, stuck closer than brothers. Stephen and Richard frequently brought my kids to see me.

Stephen and Richard were Seal Beach bachelors to the max. They weren't religious at all. They loved everybody and were gentle and loving. They may not have professed a particular faith, but they sure modeled the walk that is truly Christian.

In the 1970s, Stephen was into touchy-feely, New Age spiritualities that were way out there. He was actively involved in the Forum and the Summit, and I thought people looked up to him as one of the leaders in the movement, almost as if he were a guru.

I admired Stephen's Jewish culture. He was a disciplined man, looking and hoping for the Messiah.

But Stephen believed in me and when things got crazy, Stephen would drop what he was doing and stand by my side. He was with me through the trial.

Richard came out of the 1960s Berkeley and Haight-Ashbury culture. He was single, aloof, and very philosophical. *Like, wow.* Richard and I loved to be in Stephen's 1965 red convertible Jaguar XKE with the top down.

In the early 1980s, the three of us would smoke a little "hooch," or marijuana, and walk along Seal Beach having deep, philosophical discussions. We spent eons together out there in space.

Where were the religious people from church? The Episcopal Priest from the parish I attended was a young man in his 40s. I made large contributions to the church, and on occasion, we would take chauffeur-driven rides in WHIPCRM, my Lincoln stretch.

Forest would drive the priest and me around while we had wine and talked about world affairs. We didn't really connect with regard to spiritual things, and he didn't lead me in prayer or draw me into a deeper walk with God. Nor did this priest visit me at home…or in prison. *Cheers, buddy.*

SCENE TEN
THE EX-CON

{1985}

45
HALFWAY HOME

Day after day, I prayed: *God, bring me a Christian woman who understands that a relationship can't exist unless a couple loves the Creator first.*

At that time, I was appealing my court case. I had a court-appointed attorney, so I put my case together. On February 25, 1985, after serving five months of the initial 16-month sentence in Chino U, I was released early for good behavior. In the federal system, an inmate serves every day of a sentence, but in California's system, only 66% of the sentence is served.

I was driven—and I can assure you that it was not in WHIPCRM—to a halfway house in Anaheim, an old converted Motel 6 along Interstate 5, where I had four remaining months to serve.

In the halfway house, about 30 men were each given a bunk and a storage unit. We had to find jobs and call the house every hour. The house would call the number back to be sure we were really there. We did this every day until we were released to the parole officer. It was a lot better than prison—I was outside...but it was still prison.

I had some simple jobs. And I had a blind date, at least that's how I remember things. My friend had a date with *her* friend. I didn't want to be there, and *she* didn't want to be there, either. She broke the silence and asked me what I did.

I told her, "I wake up at 5:00 a.m. every day and pray. Then I read Proverbs, John, and James for practical wisdom."

She repeated her question, "*What* do you do?" I said, "I pray and eat breakfast." She said, "Me, too." And I said, "Hey, let's talk about God's love." And we became buddies.

We ordered iced tea, we weren't interested in drinking or sex. We talked about things that were true and good.

She didn't know I was on parole. It wasn't until the third or fourth date that she asked me, "Why are you always making those phone calls? It's weird. You call out, and then they call you right back to make sure you're there."

And I said, "Well…let me tell you a story." I shared with her about the course of events that led me to calling the halfway house every hour to check in, just to complete my sentence.

She was single. Her father had been a Marine Corps Drill Sergeant for 30 years. She was the oldest child. Never had a traffic ticket. Didn't know about bad stuff.

I believe she heard the voice of love, too. And God said, "You love this guy, right?"

And she was on a blind date with an ex-con.

46
90 MEETINGS
IN 90 DAYS

My father and mother came from a long line of alcoholics. While my father himself didn't drink, my mother did. Every one of my siblings had an addictive behavior, and I was not exempt.

It wasn't until late in my business career as an entrepreneur and film producer that mine kicked in. In addition to the requisite social drinking, I became an alcoholic.

I was literally under the control of something destructive, and yet I was unable to stop. The mind is powerful. It wanted—and *got*—another drink every time, while my will to resist became weaker and weaker.

Alcoholism kept me in the dark. Although I was drinking socially, I felt completely alone. I couldn't see that I was on my way to self-destruction and I was powerless to overcome my addiction.

By grace, the most benevolent force in the universe, the only God, sent me friends like Stephen Bruce and my new honey, Sandee, who flat-out told me, "Bud, you got a serious problem. You will deal with it *now!*"

It took the help of my friends and the loving intervention of God before I became willing to face the truth about myself. I was outwardly successful, but my nature was having its way.

I listened to the One who is the main step and surrendered my will. Then I plugged into Alcoholics Anonymous and I faithfully attended 90 meetings in 90 days. That was all it took.

Sometimes it happens quickly if the tools are put into practice, and sometimes it happens slowly, but I guarantee you, it will happen. The Spirit that gives life is the one that wants me to live life and live it to the fullest.

On the dark side are spirits, like those in bottles sold at liquor stores. These spirits want to rob, steal, and destroy. They lie. As the ancient knight said to Indiana Jones after his cohort drank from the wrong cup and aged instantly, turning to dust, "He chose poorly."

47
1-2-3, 1-2-3, 1-2-3

When I got out of the halfway house, I had no where to go. I had my surfboard and my wetsuit and a Bible and two pairs of shoes. That's all. Joy took the rest. I said, "Sandee, I get out June 29, 1985. I have no place to go."

God spoke to Sandee, *You take this boy home.* It must have happened that way because the fiercely independent, eldest Christian daughter of a Marine Corps Drill Sergeant miraculously said, "You're coming home with me."

Three months later, we got married, and that was 21 years ago. It happened as quickly and as smoothly as a fast-track race. When I married Sandee, my Grandpa Pop charged me to make sure that the first thing I did in the morning was to pray with my wife before I left the house.

He said he and Grandma prayed together every morning, unconditionally, to cover each before they left the house and started the day. If Grandpa was out of town, he called her from wherever he was and they said The Lord's Prayer or whatever came out of their hearts. Grandpa Pop left a legacy that we have followed to this day.

Three times a day, Sandee and I page each other: "1-2-3, 1-2-3, 1-2-3." This is our version of text messaging that means: "I love you, I love you, I love you." One of us sends the first code, and the other one sends it back. Every day. We're best buddies, and we stay connected through prayers—or rather, through pagers. What I prayed for, I got.

I'm looking forward to growing gray hairs so I can model love for my grandkids, Connor and Parker, ages 4 and 6 in 2006. As a grandpa, I can teach them respect, honor, and how to walk Grandpa Pop's walk.

48
A TWO-POINTER

Because the District Attorney's Office had spent over $1 million on their investigation, making my case one of the most expensive in Orange County's history, the DA put a tenacious parole officer on my case. He was determined to get something out of me.

Mr. Harbitz admittedly had a difficult job working for the Orange County Parole Department because he only dealt with the really bad people. I suspect that the DA had that parole officer do everything in his power to entrap me and then bust me for breaking parole.

The goal was to get another year out of my hide in state prison, which would look a lot better on the books than the reality: "not guilty of fraud, but guilty of a technicality!" Mr. Harbitz didn't just take my temperature, folks, he put the heat on me.

People are sent to jail in the state system based on a point system. For example, you get 500 points for a murder. If you had a weapon, it's more. If you have prior record, that's another 100. The maximum is 850 points—then you're sent to Soledad...you're a real bad boy.

Let's say it's theft. No weapon, 40 points, minus 10 points if it's the first offense. If it's a theft with no weapon, and no prior offense, you have to serve some time, but it would be minimum security at Chino West or Chino Main. You won't find any murderers there.

When it came to David Walden's offense, the court did not have a rating for it so they gave me one point. I was given a second point because I did not serve in the military. Everyone was being drafted into the Army because of the Vietnam War in 1967. I have a lazy right eye, 20/400 vision, so when I was asked if I could see the big "E," I said, "What big E?"

They classified me 4-F and I was ineligible for the draft. Many of my friends fought in the war to give me my freedoms today and I thank my God for their sacrifice.

The prison system rated me as a two-point inmate. Chino State Prison got their first two-point felon! In the State of California's history of offenders, David Michael Walden was the felon with the lowest points ever to serve time. Consequently, I wasn't a risk and as a result, I got the best bunk with the best view and the captain's clerk administrative position.

If I believed in luck instead of in divine guidance, then you could say I was one lucky guy.

49
"SIR, YOU HAVE
A HARD JOB."

One would think that as a two-pointer, I would see my parole officer, introduce myself, tell him my address, forgo drug testing, and see him once every three months, right?

Mr. Harbitz had me see him every week. He would take me into a closet-sized room and get as close to my face as the police at Chino who screamed that I was property of the state. Mr. Harbitz would try to break me—swearing at me and antagonizing me to strike back at him.

I would tell him, "Mr. Harbitz, you have to deal with drug dealers and bad guys. You must have a hard job."

He restricted whom I could see, and he told me what kind of work I could do. I was not permitted to work professionally in a corporation or as a tax consultant. None of that.

I got a "deputy dog" security job at a construction site that paid $5.50 an hour. I worked in Anaheim at the site from 11 p.m. to 7 a.m. and enrolled in Fullerton College to complete my AA degree. Because I knew a lot about entertainment, I took radio and TV classes from 8 a.m. to 5 p.m. After school, I slept five hours, then I'd wake up at 10 p.m., and all night long, I would sit in my car at the construction site doing my homework under the streetlight.

So every week when Mr. Harbitz asked me what I was doing, I would tell him exactly where I had been. I presented him with my time card from my security job along with my class attendance sheet so he could see where I was and what I was doing every minute of the day.

I also kept track of my whereabouts in a journal, posting my time every 15 minutes from the time I woke up to the time I fell asleep. I wrote daily encouragement prayers every day in the upper left hand corner of the log. I believe that when we write out our innermost loving thoughts to our heavenly Father, it does not return void. I still journal to this day.

My recordkeeping didn't seem to make a difference to Mr. Harbitz. He'd scream, scream, scream in my face, swearing profusely. *Bam, bam, bam, bam!* came the reply from Mr. Harbitz's club pounding his fist as a threat. For 30 to 45 minutes, he was in my face, trying to set me off. But because of my spiritual transformation, I had the look of calm. I didn't smile. I just *showed* him I was at peace. I sympathized with him, "You have a very difficult job, sir."

In the 11th month of my 12-month parole, the 4th District Court of Appeals reversed the case and dismissed the charges. I was found "not guilty" of the two counts. The "general intent" violation of California Corporation Code-25102 was wiped out. That made news, and the *Orange County Register* ran the story. With as many times as they had to revise their story, it's a good thing newspapers only last a day.

Now I had just gone through...well, a lot. I got a "Congratulations on your victory" letter from my court-appointed attorney, as if to say, "Get over it!" And was my reply supposed to be "Thank you"? Mr. Harbitz even did a 180° turn and started treating me well.

It seemed that I was exonerated, pardoned once and for all, and was now back to being an innocent non-felon. A prior record had just been wiped clean and I confess the sound of "not guilty" rang real *sweet* in my ear.

Of course, the judicial system hasn't quite mastered throwing sins from the west into oblivion in the east. Big Brother still requires thorough explanation to employers, creditors, and anyone in the Information Age who asks before giving me clearance, "Why is this showing up in our investigation, Mr. Walden?"

That's my cue to give the gate-keeper my *gigazip* card so the 7,000-page exoneration from the 4th District Court of Appeals can be read.

I was dismissed from serving parole in the 11th month, but I continued through the end of the 12th month. I liked Mr. Harbitz and not only wanted to encourage him, but I also wanted to completely fulfill my obligation so there would be no question that I paid my dues.

At the end of the 12 months, I was given my "Ex-con Card of Completion of Parole" and I have it to this day, in my Upper Room with the attorney's congratulation letter. But was it over?

Absolutely, I answered…at the time. The law allows for the Prosecuting Attorney, in this case the District Attorney, to challenge the 4th District's ruling. I already served time, but they wanted more.

The deal was to save The System embarrassment and for its sake, I was to accept this deal or be haunted all the days of my existence on planet earth. "So, what is the deal, boys?" Without an absolute code of ethics—say, ten good rules to live by as inscribed on stone tables—relativism can't pinpoint guilt.

It was déjà vu, and I was once again sitting in the attorney's office back in 1984 when I was given good news and bad news: "Prison, but ya scored the captain clerk job!"

Whoever the players were in the unseen corners of the playing field, and for whatever reason, a negative force was doing everything to stop me from going ahead as a light of hope who overcame despair. Some evil force did not want this human—however imperfect—to give a fellow broken soul a word of life. The oppressor was threatened by love and "doing unto others."

From the dungeons of Sacramento, the spirits excavated the one count of a general intent technicality and placed it on a desk in the DA's office. They found a vehicle for their malice.

People are durable, to a certain extent. They can take a lot of tribulation, and some will go the distance, but others will wipe out. I was compelled to go the distance with this DA and defend myself against what I now believed was spiritual warfare. I thought, "Bring it on, Mr. DA!"

There's usually a compromise when sore losers are involved. The DA wanted to charge me with a general intent securities violation, but I conceded to a misdemeanor. So I signed the settlement, and the trial was over and out. Poof! Those spirits were smoke.

SCENE ELEVEN
FOLLOW

{1987}

50
WHO WANTS TO BE
A MILLIONAIRE
...AGAIN?

I was approached by a number of attorneys who had been following my case. They saw the injustice and a clear damage suit of $40 to $50 million if I were to agree to pursue a lawsuit.

The City of Orange and their Police Department and Fraud Division made many errors that came out in the court testimony. They defamed my name, the name of my employees, and the company as a whole, causing the seven corporations to lose millions in revenue.

In essence, the City of Orange's Police Department had violated my Constitutional rights. The police fraud investigator met with my investors on several occasions and boldly stated that I had stolen their money. He told them that the movie was a big scam and would never be produced, let alone be released.

The lawyers were drooling. I would sue the City of Orange, and it would bankrupt the self-insured city. We could take them out.

We had until midnight on February 13, 1987, to file our suit, exactly one year from the date of my sentencing.

And one year was a long time, especially when people kept telling me that I won the Lottery, big time.

Lawyers estimated that we would settle out of court in three or four years for a substantial claim. We were led to believe that our share would have been $6-7 million. The lawyers would have gotten the same and probably much more.

In our prayer time, Sandee and I really believed that we would settle for millions. Sandee had a 1963 Ford Maverick, and I had an old GMC pick-up truck that was given to me by Mac. If we went forward with the suit, we would head straight to the new car lot.

After the appeals court reversed the case, word got out to my clients and all my friends came back, reassuring me, "Oh, we knew you didn't do it. Oh, buddy, buddy, buddy…." They encouraged us to sue, saying, "Look, bottom line, go for the gusto. Shoot big. You walk away with $7 million. Hey, and along the way, don't forget me—your crony who helped you out." Good thing I read about fair weather friends in the Book of Job.

But we also heard a voice that said, *Follow me.* We wondered, *Is this God speaking to us?* It was a soft voice, *I have something in mind for you. Follow me.* Yet, I confess there was another voice that persistently nagged me with the seductive promise: *Take the $6 million, man!*

When a mother calls her child, the child knows her voice, just as sheep know their shepherd's call. I flashed back to the time in my backyard when I put the 357 Magnum to my head, when the same reassuring, mysterious voice that was now telling us *follow me* said *I love you.* The voice of *I love you* was the same voice as *follow me.*

Was there a choice? Nope. He saved me then and He will sustain me now even driving Sandee's '63 Maverick and my GMC pick-up.

On the evening of February 13, 1987, the paperwork was ready to go. I had until midnight to file the lawsuit. Sandee and I stayed up all night and we celebrated, not about going to court, but about following the most judicious voice we had ever heard, a voice of the supreme Judge and unanimous Jury, a voice of the utmost integrity.

Sandee and I listened, and chose not to file a lawsuit. We practiced Psalm 137:3, "Trust and do good...delight in the Lord...commit your way...rest and wait on me." Love and follow....

God let me decide whether I would build up my spirit or my ego, and I made the decision to follow wherever the Spirit of God led. This step was a major milestone in my journey, laying another rock in a sort of Stonehenge around the miracle of February 5, 1983, when my spiritual transformation had occurred.

Have you ever been at the bottom of the Grand Canyon and looked up? Sandee and I were living the Grand Canyon experience, folks. It was 6,000 feet straight up. The obstacles ahead of us were gigantic. The challenges we had to face each day as godly, renewed people seemed insurmountable.

My family and friends thought I had gone over the edge and would never again surface. They pitied me, but only because they lost the opportunity to tap into a millionaire's pocket. They scolded: "You just passed up the chance of a lifetime!" They did not understand that my lifetime began on February 5th at 11:30 a.m. I reinstated my licenses (look ma, no felonies!), I found part-time jobs during the day and night, I went back to college, and I started serving at a no-frills, Bible-believing church.

I wanted simple faith, the kind that had to be lived out. So I got plugged into volunteering to serve in Mexican prisons, rehab houses, and with downtown homeless programs. I volunteered to work with gang kids from the inner city in a Surf 'n Study program in which I gave kids surfing lessons, then taught them practical biblical principles. I was doing good things...things that cannot be bought with six million bucks.

I had a change of course that took me in a new direction. Pre-2/5/83 at 11:30 a.m., I was a successful entrepreneur, I was after the Pot o' Gold. Post-2/5/83 at 11:31 a.m., I didn't want to *take*, I wanted to *give back* by coaching, mentoring, just helping in any way possible.

I didn't know theology. I knew Proverbs and the Book of James. "Pure religion according to the Father is taking care of orphans and widows and keeping yourself from being polluted by The System. It's getting off your butt and thinking about someone other than your stinky self, bud!" (That's my translation, and remember, I'm no theologian.)

51
DOING THE WORD

Our men picked up food from the community and delivered it to seven orphanages twice a week. One of the orphanages was operated by Carlotta and Marcos Gutierrez. Carlotta, a paralegal, and Marcos, a lawyer, were familiar with darkest Tijuana.

They not only took care of 45 children in their orphanage, but they also made consistent efforts to help prostitutes working on Tijuana's notorious main street, *Avenida de la Revolución*, by guiding them to a straighter, more respectable path.

I supervised homeless men in downtown San Diego as we collected donations for their orphanage. To show their appreciation for our efforts, Carlotta and Marcos invited me and Sandee to have lunch with them in their home. This was March 1994, ten years after Chino.

They picked us up at the border, and our first stop was their orphanage, and then we visited their resource center for the prostitutes on *Revolución*. Expecting to head straight to lunch at that point, we wondered why the van stopped in front of 30' walls where men on towers gazed down, holding automatic weapons. This wasn't part of our lunch plans.

Tijuana's La Mesa State Prison is one of the worst prisons in the world with a reputation for violence. It looked like the worst day at Chino U. For ten years, Marcos and Carlotta had been visiting Hispanic inmates inside La Mesa. They gave away food and clothing and brought good news into a bad place.

With me and Sandee still in the van, they had stopped to deliver more food and attend a short church service behind the walls. Their names were on the master list—and no one gets in without being on that master list.

Sandee and I found ourselves being stamped by the guards in several places and before we knew it, we were ushered into hell on earth. It could have been a Paramount Studios back lot scene of Sodom and Gomorrah.

Thousands of people were barely clothed, some were naked. People were having sex in dark corners, prostitutes were walking the streets, and addicts were shooting up right in front of us as we passed by—in a hurry! It was completely out of control with depraved, filthy, bleeding, bruised, and sick people. I imagined this as one of the lowest rungs of Dante's Inferno, with guards lining the brim of the blazing cauldron, stirring the demonic stew with guns.

We were escorted by two couples—one in front and one behind—into a cafeteria where 70 Mexicans were singing. They looked healthy and wore clean clothes.

We had walked into incredible light. We turned around and looked outside the cafeteria where it was dirty and dark beyond measure. I could feel its tentacles reaching towards me. I was transfixed. Awed.

While Sandee is the paranoid one, I'm the adventurous guy who always wants to see more. Carlotta and Marcos dropped off food and clothing, and then they had to push me through the front gate and out of that prison. We left for our leisurely lunch—an Emperor's banquet by contrast.

A voice in my inner spirit put words in my mouth and I asked Carlos, "Are there *Americans* in there?" "Sí, lots of

Americanos." "Dónde? Where are they?" "They are hiding." "Does an American pastor or chaplain or anyone go in and visit our Americans?" "No, no, no."

It was as if a steel bar had jabbed into my heart. I was transported back to Chino State Penitentiary where I was being hosed down on the back deck, condemned as "property of the State," and abandoned. But these Americans were in Mexico. I put myself in the prisoners' places and told Sandee, "This is not good."

Sandee looked at me, shaking her finger as she warned me, "You're not going back in there!"

All I could think about for two months was how to get on that master list.

52
ENTRADA:
THE GRAND CANYON

We went on vacation to the Grand Canyon, but we fell in. Some folks take falls in their everyday life, but they fall into a manhole or a ditch. Sure, it hurts, but they can get out pretty easily. My fall was a little more difficult, ya know what I mean? It was more like the little boy with wax wings who flew too close to the sun, and the next thing he knew, he was a meteor striking earth. Man, was his dad bummed. Poor little Icarus.

On February 13, 1987, when Sandee and I heard the voice say *follow me* and then, *It will cost you,* we looked up the side of the 6,000-foot steep walls and thought, *We have hands that work and feet that work,* so we started climbing little by little.

We were on our way up the walls of the Grand Canyon.

Climbing up the Grand Canyon's sharp, rocky cliffside is difficult, especially in that Arizona heat. The secret is to keep climbing one foot in front of the other, one day at a time. God provided the living and met all our needs—rather than our *wants.*

Sandee and I lived in a one-room apartment when we started this climb. That was hardcore rock-climbing.

After visiting La Mesa prison, I felt an urge to learn more about this God stuff. I earned my AA in Business and Communications and then went on to Calvary Bible College and earned my Bachelors in Theology and Biblical Studies.

I stepped out of the profitable business world and into the Lord's work. Instead of making a living as a business consultant for $150 an hour, I was taking on more and more hours as an ordained minister and social worker. I put in 30 hours a week as the children's and missions pastor at my church for $1,500 a month. I worked another 30 hours a week, mainly overnight shifts, at Carlsbad's Intercommunity Services, where I started at $5.15 an hour, caring for three adults with Downs Syndrome.

In addition to meeting our financial needs, the Lord arranged my work schedules so I could also study full-time in a Master of Divinity program in one of the most prestigious seminaries in the nation, Bethel University, based in St. Paul, Minnesota, with a seminary in San Diego. Before I knew it, I was enrolled.

I was determined to get plugged into La Mesa Prison, so I put out the word for people to pray to get me on the master list. The administration didn't let Americans into prison. It was hard enough to get *out*.

53
ENTRADA:
HELL

My schedule was full so I managed my time closely. But at the same time, availability and willingness to serve are key components to success. Forty days after my first entrance into La Mesa with Marcos, Carlotta, and my Sandee, I found an open window in my calendar on Wednesday afternoons.

I went back to the prison in Tijuana, stood by the back door, and my voice said to *the* voice, *I trust you and I'm here.*

I stood there trusting for 2 ½ hours until the guard for no apparent reason tapped me on the shoulder and said in Spanish, *"Entrada."* Whoa, I was in!

He stamped my arms and led me inside. It must have been like this for St. Peter when he was suddenly escorted out of prison by an angel. Well, this guard was no angel but he was unknowingly being led by a force higher than all.

That first day, I found one American, Jay. We sat down and the first thing I did was open up the Bible to Proverbs because I'm a practical teacher. Jay was hungry to know why I was there and I simply pointed to the practical book of wisdom. He said, "You'll never come back. This place is run by the devil and no outsider, especially an American, ever returns."

I promised, "Buddy, I'll be here next Wednesday. Bring some guys next time." The next week, I waited two hours outside the gate. I was still trusting the One who said, *I love you, Mikey.* The guard was not supposed to let me in because I was not on the approved list, but he did.

I found Jay waiting with five Americans he brought. Jay told me there were over 100 American men and women inside La Mesa Prison.

I returned a third time the next Wednesday and waited 30 minutes outside the impenetrable walls. The fourth time, I found 20 Americans sitting around the table with Jay grinning in their midst. The fifth time, after 10 minutes at the front gate, the guard let me right in. Go figure. I just showed up, trusting.

Americans are usually sentenced in three months, but it's common to wait six months before being sentenced. After that, it takes another 4-6 months for an appeal to be processed and returned with a reduction or a stay. If the Consulate is active on their citizen's behalf, it takes an additional 3-4 months before an inmate qualifies to be transferred to the state of origin. Otherwise, it can drag on and on for 1 ½ years.

I tried to avoid going to the media for minor infractions because I didn't trust the spin reporters put on stories, which can twist the truth into something much worse. But for obvious injustices, I did go to the media and plead my case on the news, especially if it was to bail out a frail grandpa who was arrested for trying to save money on a prescription written by an American doctor.

By now, I'm believing the voice of love I heard 22 years ago, the same one that intervened when the bullet from the 357 Magnum should have been in my brain. At this point, the voice that said, *I love you. Follow me,* spoke to me a third time, *Trust me.*

So was I going to trust this invisible guide or not? My inner spirit said, *Okay. Lead on.*

SCENE TWELVE
THE INFERNO

{1994}

54
MEAN HOMBRES

I was admitted time and time again without permission, for two months straight. (In 2006, I am in my 12th year of weekly visits. Go figure.)

I stood on a table proclaiming a message of encouragement and practical wisdom to 100 American citizens and at least 1,000 Mexicans. I was talking stories: "I was in Chino, and all I know is I got out and now I'm here." I recruited an interpreter on my fourth visit because I speak "un po-kee-toe es-pan-yol."

I wore a light blue clergy shirt with a priest's collar for two reasons. First, to protect my tush. Most bad guys in Mexico have a strong Catholic background and they revere their priest. Second, the priest's (*padre's*) collar opened the door for me to talk about the Father (*el padre*) in heaven. When someone addressed me as, "Padre," I would change the subject, "I am a father with two kids, but let's talk about the real Padre who loves you."

We connected quickly and spoke about spiritual truth, which didn't include lies they learned in school such as, "We evolved from apes." They discovered everyone has been birthed by their spiritual *Padre.*

I was witnessing the power of love literally transforming lives and circumstances right before me. Americans came to me and asked for prayer. It was all very good, supernatural stuff. All of this was taking place in the authorities' full view. Soon, I was causing a commotion, and the *Comandante*—the head honcho, *el Señor*—took notice.

He sent orders to have me brought up to his office. I had never met him nor had I seen him, but he knew me. *El Padre.*

Most of the *Comandantes* had been political pawns who were quickly replaced when the government changed hands. In general, the oil-rich Mexican government cares little for the needs of its very poor citizens who have suffered under the abuse and inhumane policies, as evident inside La Mesa Prison. Government officials have even tried to extract money from religious organizations, accusing them of illegal activity as they crossed the border into Mexico...just to bring in supplies to the poor.

As a result, the poor in Mexico perceive that America "gives and gives and gives," so millions of Mexicans illegally try to cross the border each year to escape a government that "takes and takes and takes." If caught, they are deported by the U.S. Border Patrol and then put back so they can make another attempt...and so the cycle goes.

A corrupt government isn't unique to the border just south of California. But they happened to be next door, and God made it clear that I was to love my neighbor.

The current *Comandante* had lasted much longer than the others. As I noticed the large cross hanging on the wall behind his desk, I perceived it was because he was a just leader. He was a middle-aged Hispanic man whose presence did not need to be announced. He was handsome and in very good physical shape. He spoke broken English and it was apparent he respected the clergy.

The *Comandante* sent down his lieutenant who led me upstairs. I was ready to call Sandee and tell her to "Send in the cavalry!" The *Comandante* wanted to tell me that he and his guards had been watching me for the past six years through the two-way mirror lining the prison's entryway, of which I had no idea!

I was ready to go down on my knees and plead for mercy as he began speaking in good English: "If I were a prisoner in La Mesa, I would want you to be my pastor. You do not bribe and you are consistent in your teaching of the practical word. I have seen the changes in many of those who attend your weekly services. You visit consistently and maintain an attitude of humility. You will be our *capellán* (chaplain) *a Norte Americanos.*"

So the *Comandante* was essentially knighting me as the official pastor to the American inmates. In the end, I received the official green badge, which is like an all-access press pass that gets you backstage at a show, with no questions asked. I was the first *capellán Norte Americano* to be entrusted with one. From that moment, I reckoned I had a new ministry!

The *Comandante* gave me two days a week to come in and he authorized the use of a 20' x 20' room for services and studies. I could stay four hours at a time—which was entirely sufficient for the work of love in this forsaken place.

The voice of love had said to me, *You love me.... You follow me.... You trust me....* The next thing I knew, inmates like Jason Rappacillo, sentenced to 15 years for arming revolutionaries in Chiappas and firing at Mexican *policía*, were being transformed into new men. Jason was even given an early release because of his changed behavior. He served six of the fifteen years. This is unheard of in Mexico.

I sent you to Chino Prison, but you're going to La Mesa Prison because Jason is inside. I didn't ask for another ministry. This was not planned. I should never have been let in, but I just showed up and God opened the door. I'm still going in once a week, and hundreds of *banditos* are surrendering to God. New life, futures, and hope.

55
NADA

There are 6,000 inmates, of which 300 are Americans. The prison administration only supplies a cell, food, and water. Soup for breakfast, soup for lunch, a tortilla and a cup of tea for dinner.

In the early days of the prison's history up until recently, prisoners had to pay for rent and food. If they had enough money, a prisoner could live in a condo with a Jacuzzi for $30,000 dollars a year. When I started visiting La Mesa, it was a little, corrupt city of violence.

Inmates earn no honest money, unlike the 45¢ an hour I was paid as a captain's clerk in Chino. Drugs were rampant, and there were many administrators who became rich from the illegal activities in La Mesa. Guns were available and some prisoners owned them.

No clothing. No medical attention. *Nada.* However, one inmate did serve as a dentist, pulling out teeth with a pair of pliers. Sterilized equipment cost extra.

Today, some 12 years later, the inmates are locked in their building units 24 hours a day, except for four hours of yard time a week, and two hours a week for church, and a four-hour family visit. That's a whole 9 ½ hours out of 168 weekly hours of free time in the prison city. No wonder there was a waiting list to attend church.

For the remaining 158 ½ hours of the week, prisoners shared six bunks with 20 inmates, sleeping in shifts or doubling up, staying warm by lying with one guy's head next to someone's unwashed, stinky feet. The prisoners who don't have cells slept outside on the ground with *señor cucaracha*, where the shoes they had on when they went to sleep would not be on their feet in the morning.

If it rained, prisoners slept in damp cells where the water rose swiftly. If it was cold, they froze. The hair of newly-admitted prisoners often turned gray within a week from the stress. Inmates died weekly. Every day was a fight for survival.

56
THE WEEKLY SUPER BOWL, A SERMON OF SERVICE

The story of my work in La Mesa Prison is a story of miracles. Once a week since 1994, my volunteers and I have been delivering food, clothing, supplies, and Bibles, bringing good news into a bad place, like Carlotta and Marcos Gutierrez. In a city where a faceless new moon rises every night, bringing more darkness, I want to keep shining like a full moon.

I am the only connection most American prisoners have to the United States, so it's up to me to set up each one with a post office box on the American side of the border in Bonita, five miles from the Mexican border. Friends and family are able to mail checks to P.O. Box 1288 that I pick up and deposit in prisoners' personal banking accounts, which I also set up.

We especially keep an eye on newly-admitted American prisoners who have nothing but the clothes on their backs at the time of their arrest. We notify their family and friends of the arrest and track new prisoners' movements for safety, making sure to give them a sort of "welcome package": a blanket, writing supplies, and any permitted personal hygiene products.

Ideally, I can pay a simple fine, bail them out, and they're outta there.

For the majority who remain inside, my ministry team works to make conditions bearable. I deposit a lump-sum on a weekly basis into the account of a prisoner who is willing to serve as the fellowship's representative. A modest, weekly allowance

(40 pesos, or $4.00) for each person in our fellowship pays for essentials.

No one is allowed to bring food or hygiene items into the prison. No soap, razors, toothpaste, detergent, or toilet paper. These things can be purchased inside, and this way, no one smuggles in contraband, whether it's drugs or new tennis shoes that can be sold to buy smuggled drugs.

Everything in La Mesa Prison is for sale, any item that would buy a heroin fix for 15 pesos ($1.50). Heroin was a bustling market from 1994 until the Mexican *policía*'s raid in 2002, with an estimated 3-4,000 addicts.

What does the prison administration allow inside? It completely depends upon the whim of the guard on duty at the front gate. Sometimes I'm let in with clothes, tennis shoes, blankets, and hotel bottles of soap and shampoo. Sometimes I get in with lotion and aspirin. Sometimes I get in with *nada...* but I am persistent in my weekly attempts.

At least the guards consistently let in paper, envelopes, pencils, religious books, and Bibles. It's as if the guards appreciate any help in warding off spiritual depression in that tarpit. On Christmas, we have a special dinner, and San Diego churches donate presents for children of the American prisoners back at home.

Mexican adult equivalency classes are offered, but GED classes for English-speakers were closed down in 2004. The only time that non-Spanish-speaking Americans come together is for our fellowship—our little gathering we call the American Christian Congregation. We have 80 active members (the maximum allowed by the *Comandante*) and another 50 on the waiting list.

I try to prevent former criminals—and innocently sentenced, hapless chaps—from regressing into destructive patterns. I want them to find spiritual direction and experience God even though they're behind bars. But remember, I was a businessman. I'm not abstract. I'm a "pragmatic-Proverbs-and-James" sort of guy. I teach practical lessons about survival—both physical and spiritual because it's all connected.

Our little room is the one place where Americans leave the crowded cells and chaotic yard, and are able to gather for prayer and spiritual renewal. I only get two hours for our fellowship a week. That's the sum of their time with this friend and spiritual coach.

However, I can provide them with challenging studies in practical theology, inductive study methods, church history, and in spiritual disciplines. I coach them in character development, focusing on integrity, cooperation, and truth.

To make the most of it, I redeem every moment as if I were a Super Bowl coach. The difference is that on my team, every player is first-string—a man created and loved by God. Period.

57
THE PAPARAZZI IN PRISON

CBS covered a story about my intervention on behalf of an American prisoner in La Mesa. David was the 45-year old Vice President of Northwestern Mutual Life Insurance in Wisconsin who flew out to San Diego for an insurance conference. He had prescriptions to fill and decided to find a bargain across the border in Tijuana. The pharmacy gladly sold him the medicine, but as soon as he walked out the door, the police were waiting.

David was arrested because he didn't have a prescription written by a Mexican doctor. He had an American prescription, but nobody in Mexico told him he needed to have a Mexican one too! The pharmacy sold it and took his money, though. They slept well!

As a high-paid executive, he was way out of his comfort zone, so I met with him each week, delivering enormous amounts of mail, and depositing checks in an account I set up in his name so I could buy him the essentials: food, medicine, and hygiene products. We prayed in his cell for encouragement and we read practical Scriptures to keep his professional mind focused.

After six months, I picked him up at the border and took him to my home where he called his wife, took a hot shower, and had a meal. Then we drove to the Radisson Hotel in Chula Vista where he told his story at a press conference. It was David's story that prompted CBS to call me for the A&E Investigative Reporting Series on "Americans in Foreign Prisons."

For Christmas, David sent me an heirloom given to him by his grandmother: a picture of Jesus holding a lamb. He felt I was family and wanted me to have it.

Then in July 2001, A&E Investigative Reporting, the syndicated TV series, aired a special report, "Americans in Foreign Prisons," located in Colombia, Africa, Central America and Mexico. There would be four 11-minute segments, one of them on me and my work in La Mesa Prison.

When CBS called me from New York saying they wanted to run a story on my work in Mexico, right off the bat I said, "Do you realize who you're talking to? You know I'm a spiritual guy, one of those non-denominational transformed ones? What do you want to talk to *me* for?" The producer said they knew all about me and they still wanted my story.

I said, "I'm not into show biz any more and I don't perform on stage. I have work to do. If you want to come down here, you'll have to keep up with me because I'm on a time schedule. I leave for the hospital at 8 a.m. and pick up mail in Bonita for all the inmates. I cash their checks so they can pay their rent because cells aren't free.

"I go downtown to my halfway house called Strong Tower Sober Living and pick up bread, clothes, and toiletries for the prisoners, and next, I head to Mexico Medical in Chula Vista for donated medicine and hygiene pharmaceuticals.

"After I cross the border, the real work starts. I am a man of the cloth and I bring the prisoners good news and kick 'em in the butt and coach 'em and love 'em. That's my mission. I have 100 Americans inside and they need me, so if you come, don't get in my way." (I'm three times as busy today in 2006 with nearly 300 prisoners, and a waiting list that's longer than ever.)

Maybe I should have told them not much was happening because after I described my full day, they were even more determined to come. Sure enough, A&E showed up with cameras and filmed me running around all over the place.

The crew wasn't allowed to bring cameras into the prison, but as it turned out, those cagey guys were able to bribe some guards and get the cameras inside the prison. They filmed the grim reality inside La Mesa Prison, and the investigative report aired on CBS, revealing the inside of Sodom and Gomorrah for the first time to a stunned international audience. And that was an unforgettable wake-up call.

Our segment was the only one with a happy ending, and it was also the only spiritual one. Sandee kept her eyes closed during the show.

That was a highlight. Mostly my job description doesn't include appearances on national TV.

58
IF IT'S AN ACE,
IT'S AN ACE

Even before my spiritual transformation, my natural and learned gifts were already in place, so my personality didn't change, which I find amazing. I used to suspect that a transformed-regenerated-born-againer would become some "holier-than-thou" person. But my mindset working in the prison was no different from my mindset as a producer in Hollywood. I had an objective and I was determined to meet it. Then and now.

In my business and production companies, I carried an attitude that let people know I was serious. If a person got past my three secretaries and was allowed to see me, we sat down and talked. We focused because time was money. Now ministry is my life focus and the only time that matters is *now*.

Why did Mr. B act the way he did? Why did Judas? In his case, it was divine appointment so that a man who was given 30 shekels would lead people to crucify God. And Mr. B had a reason when he came to my house and swore he would take me down. But what Mr. B meant for evil, God meant for good. I just couldn't see it then. When God said, *Follow me*, I thought, *Where? Adónde?*

Prisoners saw something in me: consistency. I was bold and courageous and didn't just talk the talk. I lived it out, bro. I turned the other cheek and kept on going. Whether it was local or across the border, people saw that I walked by faith and they followed me.

When I preach or teach, I lay it out: "This is the way it is. Don't fall asleep on me." I defy the complacency that exists within Christian orthodoxy. It seems to me that if you do your theology, you'll find that it's about following and trusting God and loving everybody unconditionally. And, whether they have rings in their noses or bows on their toes, nobody is exempt.

Tough audiences will spit in your face and you'll say, "Do you need a piece of bread? Do you want a soda to wash it down?" Don't turn away and say, "You're using foul language, I can't deal with this. Don't you have any respect? Do you know whom you're talking to?"

Welcome to the culture of the world, it's been around for thousands of years. What are you going to do, purify it like Pollyanna? You're living in a bubble. Get out of TV. That's not real.

I walked on straight ahead, calling an ace an ace. I thought of Jesus who was a consistent leader and didn't waver to the left nor right. There aren't enough leaders like him.

59
EVERYONE IS WIDOWED
AND ORPHANED

The reality is people get sick, die, play, rejoice, have fun, go to prison, get released...it all comes to pass. And whatever you do to the least of these, you do to God, even visiting God in prison.

The Gospel of Matthew tells us that when you visit "the least of these (that's Mikey), you are visiting God." That is heavy but right on. Any one of us could be put in a situation where we woke up and found our squirrelly butts in jail. We'd be hoping for someone to visit us behind bars.

Stephen Bruce and Richard Mills came to visit me in Chino Prison. Stephen is a Jewish man who is still waiting for the promised Messiah, but he *was* Jesus almost every week, along with Richard, visiting me as friends and bringing my children. When people act outside of themselves, they are practicing pure religion.

Loving God means caring for everybody, widows and orphans. We're all lonely widows searching for an eternal soulmate, and we're all orphans looking for a spiritual parent. Simple spiritual transformation is acknowledging that we fall short of God's perfection and need help.

I believe Jesus offers that perfection for us and if we take Him at His Word, God is faithful to give us a new outlook. Then we are able to see others as more important than ourselves.

But before the transformation, this just ain't so. Thinking about others first takes a radical change from the inside out. Jesus of Nazareth does that supernaturally. It's called simple faith.

Walking the steps of love, follow, trust, I fed the homeless downtown, established reading programs in public schools and chaplain programs in hospitals, and visited prisoners. I practiced simple discipline, honesty, compassion, love, encouragement, and consistency. I established spiritual service programs downtown and inside secular institutions like public schools, hospitals, and prisons.

If one follows the God of the universe, there is no reason why people of faith can't work within hostile environments anywhere on earth. By setting up leadership models for believers who work by faith, we can make things happen collaboratively, earn a living by doing so, and transform them into individuals to find light in darkness.

On the other hand, I could buy into the world and become selfish and self-directed. That was the David Michael Walden I wanted to shoot. So instead, I died to the world in a spiritual sense. Pure religion is God caring for me, the least of these.

60
DON'T SIGN
A DEATH WARRANT

Who am I? Nobody. I was born in San Diego and landed on a surfboard. I left Chino with only my surfboard on my back.

I don't know the number of men and women who leave prison with a high school diploma and within 20 years, have earned a doctorate. Not many, I'd bet. It's a death warrant to sign a job application and check the box, "*Sí*, I have a criminal record," even after you've already paid your dues.

I could have chosen to get violent when my parole officer got in my face. That would have been easy.

But I chose the courageous path and stayed disciplined and focused. I thought of my coaches. I believed I could live by faith and hope instead of by hosting a pity-party. I walked out and said, "I want to serve someone. How can I help somebody else out?"

I volunteered to work with 5-year olds, because, check me out, I'm not a pedophile. I volunteered over and over again to wash dishes at the same soup kitchens. Other ex-cons might also volunteer for the Red Cross or dig ditches with Habitat for Humanity. Press on hard with all of your faculties and maximize the potential God has given you, and don't go halfway, otherwise, why do it? Work as unto God whether you're racing, producing a film, or even serving soup because people need to eat, and while you're serving, you'll be wearing the Crown of Righteousness.

All I know is that people saw my compassion and loved me in return. They fed me, put clothes on my back, and showed me a clear direction, like the prostitute on *Avenida de la Revolución*. It happens every single time you serve. You will succeed.

Don't get me wrong. I don't just mean spiritual success. God cares about financial prosperity. People, including leaders and servants, who follow God's plan, will prosper.

There's nothing wrong with business when we have the right intentions. Jesus talked a lot about money and investing wisely because we'll be held accountable for what we have been given. Proverbs 31 describes an excellent wife as one who is never idle, but from the work of her own hands, she makes a profit that will in turn be invested (verses 10-31). Her family not only prospers, but she also has enough to help out others.

And remember what Jesus taught about the slave who didn't invest his master's money? The two slaves who made money were entrusted with more, while the faithless slave was called "wicked" and "lazy" for being afraid, and cursed with a future in outer darkness. More will be given to everyone who has a little. Material, but most importantly, spiritual wealth will result, and in abundance (Matthew 25:29).

Keep your focus on the priority of loving, following, and trusting God...being on the lookout for Mac's widows and orphans.

I'm just grateful that God made my little tuna fish sandwich the size of a whale that can feed a whole city.

Epilogue
My Life as a Wave

{California Dreamin'}

61
THE COLOR
OF HEAVEN

As soon as my head hits the pillow almost every single night in bed, I close my eyes and it's 1962. I'm 13 years old at Manhattan Beach in a 2-3' set, getting zonked. Sometimes I tune into Hermosa Beach, or Redondo Beach breakwater at 22nd Street, or La Jolla Shores as the sun shines through a wave and I see my favorite shade of green.

When the ocean is pristine, emerald with blue, that's David Walden. Emerald is heaven and that's the medium in which I want to operate. Even if I'm about to wipe out and snap my board in half or crash into the pier, I stop right there when I see that color. I tune out. It seems as though I'm touching another dimension...the time zone of Paradise.

I had an awesome session in the waves this Saturday morning with glassy, 3-4' sets. Several choice ones just sized up as I dropped in and made my way to the lip and tucked under the curl, dragging my right hand in the face of a beauty, the emerald H_2O flashed all around me as the sun beamed in and through the board, the wave, and me. I will be dreamin' on this one tonight.

Talk about peaceful times, I never have trouble going to sleep. Bingo... I'm out within 30 seconds.

62
MY LIFE
AS A WAVE

Overall, I think of life as surfing the perfect wave: a Windansea south swell, a 15-foot peak of white that curls over and slopes into a perfect line, laying out the opportunity to just drop in and fly. It's a very big wave, but also very make-able, very ride-able.

The earth moves when a 15-foot swell forms, and that's 15 feet as measured from the back—the face of that wave is 20 feet. When I take off, the peak lifts me up like an 8.0 earthquake. I instinctively drop down, leaning on the back leg, lifting the left foot, keeping the nose above, watching the middle of the board so I have the right plane.

When the nose tips down, it's pearling, and to avoid that, I stall with the right foot, and I don't physically make a hard turn, I *think* right and that brings me up the face of the wave. Then I lean forward and make my move.

I'm ¾ down the board as I turn, and then as I come up the wave, I move to the front of the board and squat. Now I'm under the lip, and picking up speed. I may get ten toes over the nose—the prime spot—and I tuck in my butt and arch my back, raising my left hand and dragging my right.

It's the perfect pose, a ballet move. I am part of the wave. I look up and see a 10-foot wall of water. And below me is another 10-foot wall. This happens in a nanosecond because

I'm flying down the face of that wave and my only thought is, *Don't fall.* I make the wave, and come over the top. My adrenalin rushes as though I've just finished a 500-mile off-road race through the desert of Mexico, only I'm drenched instead of being caked with dirt.

63
THE FOUNTAIN
OF YOUTH

I feel a sense of connection when I see a wave break and realize how far it has traveled, thousands of miles. That little wave has been out there. It has one shot to do its thing—rise, peak, break, foam, and just fade away—and that tells about my life. When I wiped out in business, $7 million or $17 trillion dollars wouldn't have been enough to rebuild that wave.

I watch those small waves that come trickling in. They touch even the smallest of lives, sea urchins, coral, stingrays, seaweed, and sand crabs. I think about my sister, Doreen. Her little life only traveled 2 ½ years before it broke into a little coffin in 1958. Now she's in heaven dancing and singing.

Some waves are huge, 25'. That's a long, impressive life a century old. Waves are old or young, but they all come to an end...and disappear. Jay and David were released from prison—maybe that's when my crest peaked. Or maybe it was February 2006 when we baptized 68 prisoners....

Tonight I may be slammed in my car and taken out, but I would be transformed by God—dressed in silks and shining like an angel rising effortlessly from the wreck, weightless and at peace.

When a wave recedes from the beach, the sand glistens. As a kid, I would take my skim board and glide across the silky water, on the glorified body of the shoreline, the hem of God's robe.

For the past 50 years, I've been surfing on my one little postage stamp piece of the ocean, sensing the connection between me, my board, and the sea.

After that much practice, you learn how to set yourself up as the wave forms. You are so outside your physical body that you position yourself as though you are one with the board and wave—lifting, lifting, lifting, you feel the very instant, the nanosecond, that the wave lifts you up and you find yourself standing on the board.

You don't *think* right, you *go* right. You flow into that wave and you're a part of creation. When you're locked into the section, and cut across the face of the wave, you're walking on water. There's no body-to-body contact, there's just connection as you become a part of the wave. It's a spiritual rather than a physical sport.

I've been reading *Surfer Magazine* every month for the past 40 years, and almost every issue mentions "the Zen of being tubed" or "the Zen of becoming one with the wave." I can understand why some surfers practice Zen Buddhism, and I draw from their practice in my relationship with a loving Creator by honoring creation. What a gift!

Surfing gives you some sense of what it will be like when God takes us out of the physical body and into another dimension. "Catch a wave and you're sitting on top of heaven..."

And for those of you who have observed my adrenalin-charged, high-energy level and asked, "Where is the Fountain of Youth?" I'll tell you. On the tip of a Phil Edwards 9'2" longboard, hanging ten toes over the nose on the face of a 6' south swell at Trestles or Rincon or Malibu or Windansea. It's all good when you have the Spirit inside you working, carving, comforting, and giving you that inner peace. You really are sittin' on top of this world...and the world to come.

According to my will, my son has strict orders to cremate my body and put my remains inside the foam of that Phil Edwards longboard, pour glass over me, and hang me on the wall so my children and friends can point to my Hobie Classic and say, "There is a cool wipe out hanging on that wall...Surf Dog Walden!"

64
MY CALVARY

It seems to be our nature to look for a wipe out—a fresh resurfacing from a deep place. When we go over the falls and find ourselves tossed around by the currents, pressed to the bottom, out of breath, then we instinctively seek the surface.

We might look up and see a surfer paddling over the crest of the wave on a board and imagine the form of a cross with windmill arms. Our only thought would be *up!*

And like a surfer who grabs the line attached to the board, we sense a power that makes us float and thrusts us into the light, bursting out of the roaring currents to grab for a new life after the wipe out.

I can imagine how Isaiah felt like when he simply said, "Woe unto me, I am a stinker among a bunch of stinkers, but I believe in a living God. What now?" And God said, "Go, go, *GO!*"

Keep in mind, if someone else walked in my flip-flops, what I might consider a 25' wall of scary stuff, to that person might be a no biggie, a 4' shore break.

When I make a commitment, it is like I'm taking off to face fear. I lean into the wave. Hesitating for even a moment could mean trouble if I was caught in the rip currents and couldn't touch the bottom and push up. So I choose to lean into life and take risks without holding back, going over the edge to face fear. It's the Creator's design to mold us in his divine currents, and if we trust him, it's all good. That's his promise.

I look at the cross and say my Calvary was there, between the barrel and the brain. I believe Jesus took it for me. Whatever he tells me to do, I show up and do it. Boom, I do it. *Yes, sir!*

Aloha for now!
Chappy Dave

Don't you see, you planned evil against me
but God used those same plans for my good,
as you see all around you right now—
life for many people.

The Message, Genesis 50:20

PART THREE
WITNESS

{Calling Stephen Bruce, Richard Mills,
and Sandee "da Boop" Walden to the Stand}

65
STEPHEN BRUCE,
SCHMOOZE OPERATOR I

My life would be so different and my story would be untrue without the contributions of three wonderful people whom I have the pleasure of introducing in these next pages.

Stephen Bruce, owner of Seal Beach Financial Center, remembers the mystique surrounding my public persona "in the day." He became my best friend, closer than a brother. Stephen told me how he remembered things:

"There was this buzz where I worked at Travelers Life Insurance Company regarding David Walden. Then I was assigned as his field representative and I thought, 'Wow, David Walden? He's a legend. He sends us so much business.'

"On my first visit to David's office, I was made to wait for a sufficient amount of time before being ushered into his elegantly appointed office. We looked at each other, shook hands, and became instant life-long friends.

"David and I would sit on the shore of Seal Beach on summer nights and have conversations that took us way out there. When we were first hanging out, David would constantly report in to Joy. It was his way of keeping himself tethered so he didn't float into Never-Never Land.

"One day David called and said, 'Do you want to go to Hollyweird?' His limo WHIPCRM pulled up with Forest driving. As we entered Hollywood, David called Forest on the intercom and the limo starts driving parallel to a good-looking woman walking along Sunset Boulevard. The window rolls down and David looks out and says, 'Whoo, whoo, lady.' That's the most aggressive womanizing I ever saw from him.

"On a ski trip to Big Bear, David sprained his ankle while hotdogging, but he still got around by hopping, always wearing his shades. Mr. Hollywood. We'd leave him in the cabin and go skiing without him. Poor guy.

"Our friendship grew really strong. That's when David pulled me aside and said, 'I need to talk to you. One day soon, I'm going to be arrested.' He explained why and mentioned the name, 'Mr. B.'

"I knew who Mr. B was and said, 'That sounds bizarre. You've been on a straight track so why would Mr. B make it crooked? What you've been doing is common practice and completely legal. He must really be angry with you to make those kinds of accusations.'

"The simplest version of the allegation against David is this: he tied together a series of private offerings. It's up to people in financial services to interpret the law, which is frequently a fine line, so David hired attorneys to design the private offerings and he felt everything was done by the books.

"But the prosecutor went after David with a vengeance. It was while David was in Europe making *OASII* that regulators entered his office with a warrant to get a particular file, and they emptied the place. This was traumatic and it shut him down."

66
STEPHEN BRUCE,
SCHMOOZE OPERATOR II

"David went through a year and a half of trials and at the end, he called me in tears. He said, 'It's over. On four counts, they found me 'not guilty,' and on the fifth count, 'no contest' because of the way the SEC indiscriminately removed files from my office.'

"David was ecstatic and it seemed like we would never stop celebrating. Then came the call I will never forget. He said the prosecutor was very upset because the County of Orange had spent more than $1 million trying to take him down, and they lost.

"The prosecutor filed a complaint with the NASD. They got David that time and sent him away to Chino Prison to pay his dues, which actually meant paying for the million-dollar trial the county lost.

"David once said to me about the sentence, 'You know what, Steve? I'm paying for my other sins. I'm not guilty of these charges tied to CCC-25102, but I am guilty of putting retired schoolteachers and others into investments that were too risky for them, even though it wasn't illegal.'

"Richard and I would visit David in Chino. The visiting area was a fenced courtyard where the inmates—tough guys—would come walking out to talk and visit with friends and family. Most of the inmates looked and walked alike.

"Then we'd see this little guy leaning forward as he hustled 60 mph swinging his arms, holding a clip board and notes.

Within a short time, David was running a Bible study group and he had become the captain's clerk.

"David was released from Chino after half of his sentence had been served because of exemplary behavior and service. After David was out of Chino, he lived in a halfway house, and then moved into a new townhouse with Sandee.

"One day while Sandee was at work, David called and asked me to come over right away. I walked in and saw the place was a mess. They were still unpacking. Open boxes and mirrors were scattered all over the floor.

"I said, 'David, what's up?' He said, 'This!' And David snapped open a beer, held it high, and poured it into his mouth so it overflowed from his face onto the floor. And I thought, *He's drunk.*

"I remained calm and said, 'Oh, so you're pouring beer all over your face.' At that point, David burst into tears and started slamming doors in anger. Then he grabbed another beer.

"David admits he comes from a dysfunctional family situation. The tendency to addiction was definitely there. I know David called me for a reason. It was as if he was saying, 'How can I stop this?' And I thought, *Who am I to stop this? He's a Christian and religion isn't even working.*

"As David was raging, I had a revelation. I told him, 'There's not a power strong enough. Certainly not me nor Richard. It's not Sandee. It's not Jesus. There's only one power strong enough to stop this.' He said, 'What?'

"I reached for a mirror leaning against the wall and I shoved it straight in front of his face. He bolted back against the wall as if he'd received an electric shock.

"When we talked a few days later, he simply stated, 'I no longer drink.'"

67
STEPHEN BRUCE,
SCHMOOZE OPERATOR III

"Me, Richard, David, and David's brother, Jimmy, put together a business, Four Growth Incorporated. There were 'four' of us, and we were 'for' the growth of other companies. David told me I should be the president even though I had no knowledge of how to be one, much less how to run a corporation—big or small!

"David had the experience. He was the key person because he had new ideas and had already been successful in business twice, becoming a very wealthy man when he was quite young—before losing everything. David, Richard, and I were broke, and we depended on David's brother, Jimmy, for startup money.

"Jimmy, our treasurer, had agreed to loan us up to $50,000, but he made a decision, *no mas*, after loaning $5,000, one-tenth of what he originally planned.

"There were family issues going on between David and Jimmy. Jimmy was angry at David because he felt that David was being irresponsible. The family feuds led to Jimmy's abrupt withdrawal.

"We learned two things. One, that the business strategies that worked years ago and today's business strategies were not quite the same thing. Two, that the money monster steals energy and ruins lives.

"If all of us hadn't been so concerned about where the next dollar would come from, we could have made it. We thought we'd all be multimillionaires with this business venture, and we probably would have if we had stuck it out. I'm sure David could have done it a third time.

"I own a sports car, a 1965 Jaguar XKE convertible. It's a man's cool, show-off car and David loved it. He called it 'The Corporate Jet.' One day in the midst of our economic depression, we were trying to close a deal at PickFair Studios in Hollywood. We decided to drive the XKE.

"We were both wearing three-piece suits. After the meeting, we found ourselves sitting in 100°F August heat on the 110 Harbor Freeway, stuck in traffic. We were stopped next to a big truck with its exhaust pipe in our faces and we were going 0 mph. Sweat was pouring down our collars. We were drenched and I was thinking, *Dear God get me out of here—this is terrible!*

"Without any prompting, David and I slowly turned our heads to face each other at the same time. David grinned and matter-of-factly said, 'This is what we're doing *now.*'

"Amazing how just a few words can deliver so much information, and I realized, *Why would I make this situation such a bad thing? In 15 minutes, we'll be driving down the freeway and it will be part of today's experience.* I often use that expression in many different versions, kind of like, '*This, too, shall pass.*'

"Before he went to prison, David almost died. In the midst of one of his worst times, he had an epiphany and heard the voice of God, of love. This created a total shift in David and he started studying the Bible.

"My fear was that I was going to lose the David I knew. David had always been David. Now, after his six months in Chino, I was afraid he would change or disappear.

"When I was in my early teens, my best friend enrolled in a Catholic seminary and I thought, 'I'm losing my buddy, he's going to become a priest. It's never going to be the same.' I felt the same concern when my ex-wife became a born-again Christian.

"I lost a few long-term clients when they become born-again. They said it was because I wasn't a Christian. I'm Jewish and they would only go to Christian tax preparers from now on. It didn't make sense to me. So ultimately, I had a negative view of the holier-than-thou Christians. I thought, 'What will happen to David?'

"But when David stepped into the ministry, he continued to be himself. He was a great example of someone who could say, 'I'm faith-based, I love Jesus, and hey, let's go surfing, dude.' He didn't disappear into a cult. I acknowledge that he's successful in a new way.

"Similarly, my childhood friend is married, and very devout, but he's not a priest. We are great friends to this day. My ex-wife and I are very close. She has not changed who she is and she loves Jesus with all of her heart.

"The last time David visited me in Seal Beach, he was relaxed and mellow. We had a BBQ. The conversation was different because it was David *and* Sandee. The manner in which David and I spoke in the past was no longer appropriate. We had a great visit and the weekend was over way too soon.

"About a year ago, my ex-wife and I spent the night at David's and Sandee's home. More BBQ—what fun! The next morning, David was up and running very early. He was wearing his collar and truly looked like Pastor David. He rushed into the room I slept in, gave me a kiss on the forehead, and rushed off.

"Some years ago, I was given a leather-bound Bible as a gift. As I am not a man who reads the Bible, I gave it to David. He carries it with him to this day, and every time he's speaking at the prison in Tijuana, he tells the story of our friendship.

"He assures me that if I ever visited the prison and was introduced as 'Stephen Bruce,' everybody would cheer because they would know the name. David's heart is so deeply entrenched in his work at the Mexican prison. The Christian part of him truly defines who he is today and who he will always be."

68
RICHARD MILLS,
ON DAVID'S POWER I

Richard Mills was another best friend who never left my side. He's a little more "out there" than Stephen. To prepare you to meet Richard, let me preface his side of the story with a quote from his book, *The Bible for Men: Women Friends and Male Power* (2005): "I genuinely love being a guy and I love everything that goes along with guyness. For me, being born male is a gift from the universe that I feel overwhelmingly blessed to have received."

Don't worry, Richard is hardly a chauvinist. He also gushes over women: "Women are wonderful creatures who make the experience of life a very enjoyable journey if we let them."

As a newly-published author, Richard was eager to tell his side of the story.

"I was drawn to David Walden. He was everything I dreamed of becoming. He was very successful, and by his mid-20s, he was a multimillionaire, even without a college degree. David had already done it all, at a young age, again and again and again—probably because he was always doing something, always buzzing. He can't stay still for a second.

"I wanted to be a writer from the time I was a kid and I wanted to get into the film industry. David had just made a film, *On Any Sunday II*. I had confidence in my intellect, but I wasn't willing to stick myself in front of people who would say, 'No.' That's what I admired about David. I wanted to learn from him how to deal with rejection.

"I met David through Stephen Bruce. I had parties at my beachfront house and Stephen invited David. When I met David, we became instant friends—bonded from the start. Whatever hat was on, whether he was a businessman or surfer, David was always a sweet guy inside. If you don't love David, there's something wrong with *your* character, not *his*.

"The stress level really intensified during the trial, how could it not? David had powerful forces after him to make him an object lesson as a captive white-collar criminal. To be on the receiving end of that was oppressive.

"Stephen and I didn't care what David had done. He had a great heart. We trusted him, and we didn't care about the rest. Still don't.

"I remember visiting David's large house. He complained that he had to downsize from his previous 'great big house' into his current 'big house.' I laughed because it was more house than I ever had.

"We remained constant, loving forces in his life and talked to him a lot. He needed somebody in his life to provide stability because he was losing Joy. She was bent out of shape and overwhelmed by the whole process.

"One day, Joy was reflecting about not knowing what else to do but leave or escape while David's life was spiraling out of control. She couldn't see herself remaining with David under these conditions.

"Within earshot of David, Joy told me and Stephen, 'He can't give it to me and then take it away.' She didn't say it with any malice at all. She meant a lot more than the Mercedes— she meant the money and the house. She meant her life.

"We visited him as often as we could, about once a week. There were times when we'd be driving by on the freeway close to visiting hours and we'd drop in, or we'd make appointments, usually after dark.

"During visiting hours, David would tell us about his captain's clerk job and how he was keeping his head low, but he didn't want to dwell on that topic. Stephen and I would pin him down and ask him questions about jail life, but David would get quiet.

"We realized that while he was outside his cell in the visiting area, we shouldn't make him relive jail time, so we didn't press him too hard. I worked in the prison industry for many years as a corrections counselor, correctional ombudsman, and currently as a correctional consultant. My dad served in the cabinets of two Kansas governors as Secretary of Corrections and was the head of the entire Kansas State Prison System.

"I had reason to worry about David's survival because he wasn't your typical street guy. I knew he could handle the psychological aspects of prison, but I didn't want him to be physically hurt by other inmates.

"I was relieved that he was so smart and kept himself busy so he wouldn't become a target. He mostly wanted to talk about planning Four Growth, Inc., our business consulting firm, and producing movies. Give David enough time and he's got his fingers in everything."

69
RICHARD MILLS,
ON DAVID'S POWER II

"After David served six months in Chino and was released on parole, Prosecuting Attorney Orms tried to get more out of him. Orms made it something personal.

"I suspect that David triggered or personified a previous experience and Orms went after him as though it was the past event. The judge was fed-up with Orms and realized the charges were irrational, so the judge told the prosecutor, 'Leave this guy alone!'

"David and I became much closer after his release from Chino. That's when we had time to really bond. While on parole, David was automobile-challenged so he was dependent and stayed around home, or got rides. I was going to school during the day and working at nights so I was free to hang out with him in the afternoon.

"When Sandee was at work, we'd smoke pot. David kept a stash and we'd take the pipe out to the back patio and talk about God and the world. The vast majority of our conversations were spiritual, but not religious.

"Much of the stuff that David and I were formulating at the time ended up in my book, *The Bible for Men*. We talked about business and our dreams for five, ten, and twenty years down the road.

"The nicest thing that happened to David—apart from me and Stephen, of course—was Sandee. Although during his marriage to Joy, there had been affairs because of their mutual built-up resentment and animosity, and despite the mild flirting he would do at our beach parties, David is the marrying kind. He went from Joy to Sandee.

"Sandee didn't judge him, she just took him in. It doesn't get much better than that. While our conversations were spiritual, Sandee led him towards religion. She was a strong Christian influence and she pulled David into that world.

"Ultimately, David needed someone like her because he's a strong personality, and she was a powerful influence. But I guarantee you that she didn't know we were sitting on her back patio with a pipe. David often expressed guilt about doing this on her property because he knew she'd be very unhappy about it.

"Four of us—David, his brother, Jimmy, Stephen, and myself—started Four Growth Incorporated. David wanted Stephen to be the president because of his schmooze. David would go out and get business and throw it at us, and Stephen and I would take care of it from there.

"Our backing ran out when Jimmy pulled his money, and then we couldn't survive. A psychic friend told me that if we had stuck it out another six months, we'd have it made. I'm sure we would have, but at the time, six months without much income seemed like forever.

"During the first few years after his time in prison, numerous business disappointments forced David into unprecedented times of introspection. His second time around in business, David would give deals a tremendous amount of energy and then they wouldn't pan out.

"It would happen again and again and again. His financial resources and professional backup support were usually so limited. But ultimately I feel the universe set up enormous roadblocks that were deflecting David into other directions.

"He decided to put his energies into his ministry. One day we're talking about *business*, and the next day it's all about *Jesus*. The more he got involved with Sandee, the less we saw of him.

"We saw the transformation—and the struggle—occurring. He started going to church in Orange County. He began talking more and more about spiritual things, and saying 'Praise the Lord' and 'Hallelujah.' The major transition happened when David and Sandee moved to Vista.

"I was concerned with David's faith because I came out of Kansas, the Bible Belt, where I observed extremely dogmatic, evangelical fundamentalism which often took the form of brainwashing and hypocrisy. You talk about fundamentalism that was very cult-like.

"The same people who taught us, 'The world is flat,' now tell us, 'Evolution is wrong.' I have no problem accepting intelligence behind the current scientific understanding of evolution because I can easily see it. Recorded history reveals tremendous evolutionary progress in the last 3,000 to 2,000 years and even the last 100 years alone.

"But many of the people who run the faith-based Christian and Catholic religions still tell us that we shouldn't think differently or explore, that we shouldn't use condoms, that women can't be members of the clergy or assume positions of social leadership, that ostracizing and discriminating against minorities and gays is appropriate behavior.

"These are the same people who are now trying to force us into accepting their version of Intelligent Design, the same people who taught me not to explore anything other than what they taught me.

"I tried so hard to escape that world and change my spiritual life from 'religion' to 'seeking a connection and a personal relationship with spirit.' All of a sudden, David is talking like people from the world of the Bible Belt I left behind, and it scared me to death."

70
RICHARD MILLS,
ON DAVID'S POWER III

"In my recent conversations with David, I started to notice that he emphasized relationship over dogma. Once I even I made the offhanded comment that a personal relationship with spirit always trumped biblical text and teaching, which caught him off-guard. The way I stated it could have easily been taken as blasphemous. I needed to see his response.

"When David replied that he would think about the idea, I was relieved to see that his mind was still open. I knew that he was finding his way, building his own spiritual relationship, and sharing it.

"Having worked so hard to leave the inflexible dogma of the religious world behind me, I saw that David wasn't brainwashed the way I had felt I had been by fundamentalism, and this made his new venture okay with me.

"Although David's business confidence was shattered, I suspect that David isn't done as an entrepreneur. Some part of him thinks he is, but all it would take is the right opportunity to turn him back on and he'll be there. It would be a good thing. The more affluence you have access to, the closer you can be to the people you love—you have more freedom to create.

"I'm interested in creating a men's channel, maybe a singles' channel for both genders, a spiritual and philosophical version of Spike and Lifetime. It would be very male-friendly, addressing the modern challenges that males face.

"I would create and produce the shows for that channel, and David could be very involved in it. I have no doubt that our dreams, which are so parallel, will pull us back together in the physical realm.

"All I need to do is look in the mirror, and I see David. We have a deeply-rooted historic and spiritual bond, so geographical distance and the length of time we've been apart is meaningless. David is like the family member who happens to live out-of-town. He's my brother who's away doing something else. And he doesn't do anything halfway.

"I once started writing David's life story myself and called it, *The Transformation of David Walden*. It could happen again."

Richard read and approved the transcription of this interview, and he still planned to offer more comments on my character, especially concerning women, and about people who disappeared when I went to prison. But this bittersweet interview was completed just months before his sudden death at the age of 52 while on his national book-signing tour. I will miss my brother, Richard Mills (1953-2006).

71
BOOP BOOP DA BOOP I
MISS ORANGE COUNTY MEETS
MR. ORANGE COUNTY-PAIN-IN-THE-BUTT
{Scene: Coco's and a Halfway House}

Let me step aside and give my adorable wife, Sandee, the spittin' image of Betty Boop, center stage.

"We have two different versions of how we met. David thinks we were on a blind date. But actually, I was sitting in Coco's diner one day relaxing with a hot chocolate, and mutual friends bumped into each other and happened to introduce us.

"At that point, I had been single for the past ten years, after being divorced from a 7-year marriage. I never even had a roommate because I was just fine on my own, thank you. It took me years to recover from a dysfunctional match and get healthy after my divorce.

"But it also took me years to recover from being raised by my father, a Marine sergeant for 30 years and quite the dictator. Every morning, we had to make our beds by military standards, not leaving a single wrinkle or fold, or I'm certain we would never have been allowed to eat breakfast.

"And when our family was driving in the car, my father would announce, 'No talking or laughing.' Both of my parents would smoke and the three of us kids would sit in the backseat, nauseated, trying not to vomit.

"This wasn't just on his bad days, it was every day. Whenever one of us kids couldn't take the silence any longer and laughed, my dad reached back and in a grand sweep, slapped all three of us.

"I was convinced I could never have a healthy relationship with a man again. As a divorcee, I only dated older, rich men. I thought I was Miss Orange County, the coolest thing. So when David walked in with a friend and joined us at our booth, I thought, 'Who is this jerk wearing sunglasses in a restaurant? Mr. Orange County-Pain-in-the-Butt, that's who.'

"David was not my type—he appeared to be pompous and worldly, which probably meant he enjoyed women and parties. In his defense, it's a life I didn't know, and didn't want, thank you! He was my age, but he looked younger than me—maybe it was his enthusiasm and childlike innocence.

"So we were stuck sitting together, and finally made small talk. He asked me what I did and since I didn't have anything to lose, I told him straight out, 'I'm a Christian. I wake up and have a Bible study. What do you do?' He said, 'Christian. Same thing.' The thought crossed my mind that we might just have something worth talking about.

"Later David called me and asked me out—back to Coco's—and I thought, *Why not?* At the booth, David kept excusing himself, but I was naïve and suspected nothing. I found out later that evening that he was calling his parole officer to check in.

"On our third date, David continued to excuse himself from the table, and he finally shared, 'You kind of need to know who I am.' He told me about prison and parole, but I was clueless as to what that really meant. After all, I never had a speeding ticket or stepped foot inside a jail.

"I know God was in our meeting because my heart accepted him totally, without hesitation, and it seemed like I was hearing a missionary's story, which I was. My heart went, 'Wow!' And before David returned to his halfway house, we said goodnight in the parking lot. David kissed me and I melted. I had prayed for a Christian man in my life, and here he was. I felt electricity—it was clearly God's work.

"All God had to do was show me David's spirit, which is the sweetest thing in the world. David's spirit has the eternal quality of child-like innocence in spite of all of all the ugly stuff he went through and in spite of the worldly stuff he lived.

"In a photograph I saw of David, he is looking into the camera, standing next to his daughter, but looking like her brother, looking like a child. I didn't hear pretty things about his flamboyant past, but through it all, there was this little Mikey spirit inside that cried at the drop of a hat.

"I'm a hard taskmaster and here God brings me a sweet-spirited man. His spirit wasn't ugly, negative, or bitter as one would expect of an innocent man placed on trial and then sentenced to a prison term. He could have been left foul-mouthed, but today, I'm the one who has to watch my mouth—I was raised by a Marine."

72
BOOP BOOP DA BOOP II
THE DIVORCEES MARRY
{Scene: Home}

"We fell in love overnight and we knew it. By the time David was ready to leave the halfway house, he had nowhere to go. I have this co-dependent side that tries to save everyone and fix anything that's broken, so I told David he could move his stuff—basically a surfboard—into my place.

"My first thought was not, *Does living with a man please the Holy Spirit?* but, *Do I really want someone else in my home?*

"Three months after he moved in, he got on his knee in the kitchen and proposed to me saying he wouldn't just live with me, he would marry me. In God's eyes, we were married that day in my kitchen. We had both been praying about our situation and knew it was meant to be.

"All of a sudden, I have this insane lifestyle. David was sued again for one million dollars. Then we found out from an attorney friend that we had the opportunity to sue the City of Orange since David won his appeal and was given an 'oops-sorry-we-destroyed-your-life' letter.

"We could have settled for as much as $30 million, and our share would be about $7 million of that. We were broker than broke, but we looked at each other and knew God would get us beyond this. David didn't want to relive the nightmare, so we passed on the chance to make millions. Little did we know God would honor us for that choice.

"David tried to go back and make money in tax and financial planning, but doors kept closing. We'd cry in frustration because we knew David had done it before and become a multimillionaire, but it wasn't working this time. And we would pray, seeking God's direction and confirmations about what to do.

"One day, after we crashed and burned, we sat down and wrote out our budget and came up with the amount we needed: $5,054.

"The very next day, a check arrived from a consulting firm to retain David and the amount was $5,060. God knew we needed to make the move and change direction so David would go into the ministry, and He has done this more than once since then.

"The meaning of 'wipe out'—moving from physical rags into spiritual riches—really has its roots in our home.

"As newlyweds, it was a struggle for David to keep his balance because he was so emotional. He was trying to find ways to get strong and rebuild his life, but he fell into the old patterns and used the old crutches.

"David was a recovered alcoholic but had started drinking again. I told him to get sober or get out. With God's help, David went to therapy and did become sober.

"Later, after business plans fell through, I started seeing personality changes in David. One day when I asked to see what was in his fanny pack, I found pot. I threw it out the window and almost ripped his face off.

"I told him, 'Listen, you need to understand, if you want to go to jail, it's your life, not mine. That's a fact of life.' That old Marine upbringing was hard to shake!

"And that was the end—it was finished. God lifted the addiction and to this day, David is on fire for God, or, as they say, drunk with the Holy Spirit.

"We started attending Calvary Escondido, where I noticed a flyer on the table for Calvary Bible College. As it turned out, school started the next Monday, and that's what God wanted David to do. God needed David to be out of the world, out of business, away from temptation.

"God plucked the entrepreneur out of business saying, *No, David, you don't get to be in the world anymore. I need your energy and fearlessness to be a visionary for me.* That's all God asked of us: *Begin again, and trust in me.*"

73
BOOP BOOP DA BOOP III
THE UNLIKELY COUPLE
LEARNS THE BASICS
{Scene: Forever in Process}

"I had to work two jobs to pay for his school. And then to support his ministry, I kept working to earn benefits. Through the years, we saw God's hand in David's path. After becoming a pastor, job offers in ministry kept coming to him. He didn't even have to put out a resume.

"I believe the discipline and focus I learned from my dad is what keeps us on track. I was taught prevention, to plan ahead and budget, to survive well. I was the missing piece David needed in the process of forging a healthy life—the piece he hadn't been taught.

"But in our day-to-day lives, I go overboard in my compulsiveness, following him around the kitchen while he's cooking with my spray and wipes, cleaning up his spills until he tells me to get out of the kitchen. I'm not the most gracious person. I can be so bossy, but David gets in my face and tells me to lighten up. We complement each other perfectly.

"I looked into my past, and tore myself down, but David thanks and honors me. He wants the best for me. He has taught me to live and has given me balance, and the added physical bonus is that I don't have high blood pressure like my dad.

"I've never been so psychologically connected to someone. I can be so mad at David, and think he's the biggest pinhead of a surfer with no common sense, yet there is this thread in my heart, and I'm just connected to the man.

"Since we can't always talk during the day, we page each other with encouraging messages in numeric codes to keep us on our toes about praying for one another.

"Through the years in our marriage, we have learned that for survival, laughter has to be #2 in line next to God as #1.

"We have two magnets on our refrigerator. One is a little boy in a cardboard box that says 'The stupid factory, that's where boys are made.' The other one is a little girl standing with hands on her hips that says, 'Girls are bossy.'

"Any time one of us is acting up, the other one can put the appropriate magnet on the front of the refrigerator. Then we usually start laughing hysterically.

"We are so different from each other, and probably from most couples. God brought this unlikely couple together—we didn't. The power of God and the release of laughter keeps us forever in process, but together in His love."

Part Four:
Postscript

{How I Made Millions
in the 1980s}

Disclaimer:
Do not try this in the 21ST century

74
KEEP YOUR EYE ON THE DOLLAR:
THE FULL CIRCLE CONCEPT AT WORK

Round and round the dollar goes, where it stops, no one knows.... We operated like magicians passing around an elusive coin that was hidden under one of three cups on a tabletop. No one's eye could outmaneuver our sleight of hand.

Point to where you think the coin ends up, and it's not there.

Orange County Tax & Financial Planning was known for its creativity, applied one client at a time. I developed the concept of threading the dollar for maximum yield and benefit. We were threading one dollar through four investment vehicles, each one with a tax benefit and potential for growth above inflation.

I coined the term "Full Circle Concept" to describe our objective: take "one dollar" (actually, the first $1,000 note), and work it through several channels. First, the cash value life insurance. Second, a fixed interest rate tax sheltered annuity. Third, a fixed interest single premium deferred annuity (SPDA). And fourth, an interest in a real estate limited partnership.

Once the first year cash value is credited to the policy, the investor borrows the maximum funds. The funds from the insurance contract are used to funnel through a qualifying employee's paycheck—in a dazzling move our clients loved the most, called "converting net to gross"—to purchase a qualified TSA. Would you believe that a few insurance companies had this provision in their contracts? Seeing an opportunity, we jumped on the provision and did the same thing again, borrowing from the TSA and purchasing an SPDA. And who's to say we couldn't do it a fourth time? No one.

So with funds borrowed from the SPDA, we plugged this original dollar into the limited partnership that might have owned a 16 unit apartment complex in Anaheim. The client could go right over and see their property after they wrote the check to our company. Our commission was fairly small on each sale, but we sold a lot of a little thing, so when we added up all those small slices, they formed a whole pie. Four vehicles, but only one investment.

Is your head spinning yet? Even for financial planners, financial planning isn't a simple process. But it can all be traced to $1K, "the first dollar" that began the whole process. Now take a breather, and then turn the page.

75
ONE MORE TIME AROUND
THE FULL CIRCLE

We would invest clients' funds into high cash value insurance products or annuities, as well as in limited partnerships in income-producing residential and commercial properties. (Higher risk vehicles such as motion pictures were only offered to individuals who met rigorous SEC requirements.)

The main insurance company we used was Beneficial Life Insurance Company of Salt Lake City, Utah, whose single premium deferred annuity was a jewel for investors. Travelers Insurance, U.S. Life, and Jackson National Life Insurance also had plans with high cash values and flexibility for the insured.

These annuities usually had small sales commissions. My competitors didn't sell life insurance because the commission to the agents was so low, but I wanted a win-win situation for my clients. So I generated multiple "low" commissions that resulted in overall profits for the teachers, salesmen, my companies, and for myself as the general partner.

Investors had the provision to immediately borrow from the first year's life insurance premium, and still keep the death value in place, minus the amount of the loan. So with a $1,000 deposit into the premium of a $100,000 policy, the cash value was high in the first year. Then client borrows $950 from the life insurance policy and works it through many channels of the Full Circle. If the client dies, the family gets $99,050 instead of $100,000. No biggie...just don't die.

Next, I have the client start a tax shelter annuity (TSA) through their employer. Teachers, state, and federal employees qualify for these retirement savings plans, or payroll deductions, and put up to 20% of their gross salary into a TSA. For a client who takes the full 20% out of a $5,500 paycheck (gross amount), we would put away $1,100, but the net take-home adjustment would be $950. Uncle Sam just helped us make $150 off the top.

Now the client has the $950 borrowed from the life insurance premium in addition to $1,100 in savings. The take-home pay is the same, and the savings is increased by $100, minus the initial $1,000 to purchase the insurance policy that started the "Full Circle Concept."

Here's what the client has so far: a $100,000 life insurance policy, and $1,100 in my fixed annuity savings account.

Now we put the third formula into action. Some of the TSAs allowed us to borrow against that TSA. We could borrow $1,000, leaving $100, and put the $1,000 into a real estate investment trust (REIT). You have $1,000 working in the REIT when you participate in the partnership of a little apartment complex. The real estate in the 1970s and 80s was accelerating. We would hold apartment complexes for a year or two, increase the rent, then flip the capital gain tax, and double our clients' money. Their $1,000 just became $2,000.

Then we'd take that dollar and put it back into the annuity so we didn't owe that on the TSA. It's repaid. And no one ever pays back a loan on a life insurance policy—it's a death benefit with cheap interest.

76
COMMISSIONS...
SWEET!

The customer is one happy customer. And I'm the general partner, the real estate broker, and the general agent. My agents and companies have just made a commission on the cash value (whole life) insurance policy, the tax sheltered annuity (TSA), the single premium deferred annuity (SPDA) and the real estate limited partnership. And it all started with one dollar, $1K.

An investment of $100,000 generated somewhere between 5-28% (or $5,000-$28,000) in fees for the company. Insurance products like life insurance and annuities ranged from 5-15%. Typical whole life insurance products paid as much as 75% of the first year premium to the General Agent, but I chose lower commission, whole life insurance products. They served our purposes by offering the full death benefit and high cash values up to 95% in the first year for use in the Full Circle program.

Commissions from real estate, limited partnerships, and property management paid to the company were dependent on the type of investment being offered. Real estate commissions were 6-10% while film and TV properties were between 10-25%. The fees charged in a film product usually included costs off the top for administration, salesman fees, advertising, and promotion.

There are high risks for the general partner/executive producer in motion picture projects. This decision-maker had to be a visionary leader and perform at the highest level in financial, legal, and marketing decisions. Therefore, because the successful general partner/executive producer took higher risks and also was responsible for overhead and promotion, the GP in a film partnership demanded higher fees than that of a General Agent in an insurance agency. In a $5 million film partnership, our company would make 5% (or $250,000) which would be divided three ways to pay for overhead, promotion, and me.

The companies earned management fees from the gross dollars invested. From ten clients investing $100,000 each, our various corporations could generate as much as $300,000 in operating revenue. For the most part, the overhead was administrative. The tax planners and insurance agents were commissioned based on income derived from sales of products, earning an average of $60,000 a year, which would be around $120,000 today. The tax manager received a small salary, and the securities supervisor got a base salary plus commission. Secretaries were paid $1,200-1,500 a month, which is equivalent to around $3,000 today.

The fees paid the overhead for all the companies and provided the staff with excellent benefits and my family with a very comfortable living. In addition to serving as president and CEO, I was the general partner/executive producer of over fifty limited partnerships in real estate and entertainment properties. All it took was a high school diploma and one year of junior college—and the ability to be a multitasking leader.

(These limited partnerships were my "side jobs" that entitled my family to extra bonuses and vacations that made going for it worthwhile. Mac was proud of his son-in-law.)

77
INVESTING IN THE CAN:
EITHER YOU WIN…
OR YOU WIN

I was the general partner of numerous California private placement offerings commonly called "limited partnerships." The characteristic of these investment vehicles was their limited liability, high potential for profit and generous tax benefits in most offerings. The risk for any unsecured investment is always present.

My organization stayed with more conservative investments in real estate like commercial or residential multiplexes. Entertainment properties, like films and TV, were outside the conservative investment box. The higher-risk investments required the investor to meet standards of risk tolerance, and each of these investments had to be screened carefully by a board of attorneys, CPAs, and investment advisors. Our tax planners had to examine each case thoroughly to see if the client qualified according to IRS, SEC, and corporate codes. The guidelines for film and TV investments were strict.

We formed private placements with ten or fewer investors. Many of these limited partnerships involved motion pictures and TV productions, which had certain tax benefits. For all of the films we made, we never had to advertise for investors. We found them within our affluent Orange County client base. Many of these clients qualified for investments with higher potential returns and tax incentives—in other words, investments with higher risks. The film, *On Any Sunday II*, was a project that had potential because of its successful forerunner, in addition to the stars and expert production team. It was an easy sell to investors.

Once a film was produced and "in the can," it was eligible for the IRS Investment tax credit. Therefore, 10% of the cost of the asset was a direct, "dollar-for-dollar" credit against federal taxes that was passed on directly to the investor. Plus, the life of the film, or "the can," is fairly short, so we could use aggressive depreciation and write-off a large percentage of the investment.

For an investment of $50,000 or $100,000, clients could not only write-off the amount they put in, but as much as 200% of the investment could be adjusted off the taxpayers' gross income (subject to IRS rulings on certain income/capital gains/losses). Obviously, this was in the early 1970s, so I don't advise anyone to try this at home without a licensed professional or two looking over your shoulder and signing on the dotted line below your name. That's why they charge big fees.

Through careful analysis of tax strategies based upon the legal "loopholes" of the current year, we could determine tax credits or adjustments. For example, someone in a 50% tax bracket (combining the Federal and State rates) would put $100,000 dollars in an investment. With a total of 200% in their first year "paper losses" (depreciation or allowable expense items), we would adjust their gross income by $200,000 and claim a tax credit of $10,000. This resulted in a potential gain exceeding the original investment.

The return was given whether the film was a blockbuster or a bust and the client wouldn't lose a dime. Instead, they would recoup a majority of their investment in tax savings. And my organizations earned commissions off the $100,000...*sweet!*

78
GOTCHA!

After a few years, the companies had their "Ah, ha" moment and realized what creative tax and financial planners were doing within their product guidelines. So they changed their provisions. The legal language no longer allowed the owner of an investment to borrow "tax qualified money" that would be paid to the salesman as a full commission, leaving the company with a note and no cash. The companies filled the hole and no more loop. *Darn!* But while the Full Circle was rolling in the 1970s and early 80s, Orange County Tax & Financial Services and our clients were rolling with it.

We understood those "loopholes" in the 1970s and 80s institutional system. "Loophole" is a lay term describing a legal or tax strategy and the successful know-how to implement a methodology to gain some benefit from its discovery.

Everything was legal according to the current tax laws of the day. My attorneys were busy filing the due diligence so that our organization carefully stayed within the guidelines spelled out in our contracts, carefully dotting our *i*'s and crossing our *t*'s, like Grandpa Pop taught me. There was no need to do anything outside the parameters of business. We had plenty of room inside.

Had our companies continued, we would have gotten creative in other ways and found another loop. Little did I know that an even more creative loop lay ahead, and it wasn't a short cut across the desert at the Baja 500. It was the freedom written in bold letters on the fans' hand-drawn signs throughout the stadium, and the first thing I read in my new life: *John 3:16.*

Printed in the United States
59458LVS00003B/145-195